Heaven Knows, Kate

Heaven Knows, Kate

Thomas L. Are

MOREHOUSE BARLOW
Wilton

Morehouse Barlow Co., Inc.
78 Danbury Road
Wilton, Connecticut 06897

ISBN 0-8192-1347-0

Library of Congress Catalog Card Number 84-60625

Composition by The Publishing Nexus Incorporated
1200 Boston Post Road, Guilford, CT 06437

Printed in the United States of America

To
CECIL B. MURPHEY
without whom this book
would never have been written.

And he said to him, "Truly, I say to you, today you will be with me in paradise."

(Luke 23:43)

So faith, hope, love abide, these three; but the greatest of these is love.

(I Cor 13:13)

Contents

Introduction
Heaven Knows, Kate

"I can't believe it," her voice quivered. "Yesterday he was fine. Drove the kids to school. Now, the doctor says he may not make it."

It was to be a simple surgery, but complications set in. I felt I had to say something. I was her pastor. Touching her on the shoulder, I said, "Kate, God will not let Charles die!"

How could I have made such a promise? I hoped Kate wouldn't sense my desperation. "God won't take a twenty-seven-year-old father of two children. You'll see," I kept saying, "everything is going to be fine." Kate could only cry.

Four hours earlier things had turned worse for Charles. He was barely conscious when I entered the room. Her voice hardly audible, Kate greeted me. "Thanks for coming. He is so sick."

"He'll be okay," I said.

We could hear Dr. Holder issuing orders. "Pack him in ice. We must get his fever down!" And I knew how shallow my reassurances sounded.

"Charles, honey," the south Georgia nurse said in a high-pitched voice as if Charles were a child, "we've got to give you a shot now, okay?"

I could see his limp eyes through the foggy oxygen tent. His fevered head rolled back and forth across a damp pillow. I backed away as the nurse rushed in with ice and towels. Moment by moment, the tempo around Charles' bed increased as doctor and nurses raced to challenge the inevitable.

Finally Kate mumbled, "I've got to get out of here. It's a nightmare!" I followed her into an empty waiting room. The quiet darkness offered us a peaceful retreat. For long minutes we both stared at the tiles in the floor, thinking only about the painful drama we were trying to escape. Again, tears filled her eyes.

"He's going to be all right," I said several times. "God won't let him die, just keep on believing." At that moment, Dr. Holder came in.

"I'm sorry," he whispered. "We did all we could."

Kate sank back into her chair. I waited for her to scream. Instead, she whispered, "How do I tell two kids that their daddy is dead?"

"Heaven knows, Kate—I don't know." I had nothing to say. If only I could call back what I'd already said.

Now, twenty years later and after having attended the drama of death a hundred times, I have something to say. *Heaven Knows, Kate* expresses more than my frustration of not knowing. It affirms by faith that because God knows, I don't have to know.

Also, I have in mind another Kate, a dear friend dying of cancer. Her hope was in the words of Jesus to His dying friend, "Today, you will be with me in paradise." Therefore, I think of this book's title without the comma—*Heaven Knows Kate*. And, because God knows Kate, He cares, and because He cares, He speaks. He promises her a paradise.

But she was not there yet, in paradise. What about the now, while she waited? For her interim, I have something to say about faith, hope, and love. Kate, in turn, had questions, feelings, and expectations.   P. 35

I also write with me in mind. And you. For "those of us about to die" includes us all. If you find an ounce of comfort here, for you or for one you love, my purpose is accomplished.

1
Cry
Tears are Among the Best Prayers

The phone rang. "Come quick, there has been an accident."

As a pastor, David Wood frequently received such calls. This one was different. This one involved his wife.

Twelve minutes later David parked his five-year-old Chevy in the space reserved for ministers. He leaped from his car, not looking back to see if the door closed behind him. Heart pounding from fear, he ran for the doors marked "Emergency." They were waiting for him inside.

"I'm sorry," the doctor said, "we did all we could." Beth was dead on arrival. According to the ambulance attendant, a car ...

David's mind stopped listening. He thought he would choke. Beth gone! Please, God, no, his heart cried. How long he stood there, detached from the sounds around him, he didn't know. Someone touching him interrupted his thoughts. Suddenly he became aware that the doctor was shaking his hand.

"Perhaps," the doctor said, "some of your members will be with you soon." David wondered why a common gesture like shaking hands felt so strange. But he's right, David thought, some of my members will be here soon. He waited. You must be brave, he reminded himself. The congregation will be watching you now and you must set an example of trusting God's will. He straightened his tie.

At the funeral on Wednesday, David listened to every word without a tear. On Sunday, he preached. "I am confident that Beth lives on with her Lord and I wouldn't have her back for a moment.

She has won her reward." Some left church that morning saying, "What faith!" But others said, "What a fool!"

Two months later, David cried for the first time. The doctors called it an emotional breakdown.

For over a year now David has been unable to cope with life and he still sees a psychiatrist regularly. Like many others, David thought dry eyes were a sign of faith. But he just couldn't keep up the front. He kept remembering old, unresolved arguments and words spoken in anger. As long as Beth was alive, they could talk things out. He could express his love for her and his anger. But now she is gone. Feelings of guilt haunt his brave smiles.

David has failed to understand that mourning brings its own healing. He would have done better to shout at God or cry out in pain rather than remain calm and dry-eyed. Emotional explosions may be illogical but they are normal and healthy. On the other hand, pent-up feelings block healing. Like letting off a head of steam, mourning eases pressure. Just organizing our grief well enough to put it into words often tames it.

From time to time, a friend will come to me just to talk. He will be struggling with an inner burden. So I listen. He talks for an hour, rambling on illogically, bringing up little bits and pieces of past experiences. Then, just as abruptly as he started, he stops. "Thanks," he says. "I feel a lot better. You helped me by listening."

During the entire hour, I have hardly said a word. The healing has been in his expression of feelings, not in my answers.

Yet, often well-meaning friends will not allow us to express our feelings. After a funeral one day I put my arm around a husband's shoulders and whispered, "Jim, I'm sorry." His face wrinkled and his eyes began to fill with tears.

Immediately, a sister-in-law rushed to his rescue. "Now, Jim," she said, "you stop that. You know Diane wouldn't want you to grieve this way." She went on to remind him of the brave front he owed the children. Then she left him dry-eyed and in control of himself. Jim became too brave to mourn.

Another time, in an intensive care waiting room, I sat with Jane, an anxious young wife. The doctor had just taken away all hope that her husband might survive. She began to lose control and cry. A friend immediately took charge. "You must not behave like this," he scolded, "you have faith. Trust God and everything will be all right."

She railed back at him, "How can you say that? My husband is dying. Nothing is going to be all right. If God is loving, how can He do this to Bill?"

I was glad to see her express anger with her friend—and with God.

Jane had never in all her life doubted God's goodness. So how else could she have reacted to this unexplained suffering but with the feeling that God had deserted her? Her anger reflected more faith than would have been shown by quiet resignation. At least, she took God at His word in believing that He cared. She accepted the full impact of her tragedy. "How can God do this," she cried, "when I trusted Him to take care of us?"

If she had expected God to be cruel, she wouldn't have been confused. Her anger actually reflected her faith. Because God loved her and she knew it, she felt betrayed. Being a Christian did not lessen her pain of grief or her need to mourn.

Grief hurts. It brings with it feelings of guilt and loneliness. It agonizes the mind and nearly stops the heart. Grief gives birth to emotional and physical pain. No wonder we often try to deny it in ourselves and feel uncomfortable with its presence in others. "You must be brave now," we say. Yet grief comes to all of us as an inescapable part of life.

The only way to avoid the pain of grief is to avoid loving, for the price of love is sorrow. No matter how sweet the joy of it, love is accompanied by the realization that it cannot last. Incompleteness mars the greatest love. Some people play it safe by refusing to get too involved with anyone.

A family said, "We'll never have another dog in this house. It hurts too much to lose them." They try to avoid grief, but it won't work. They may divorce themselves from pets but not from other people. God created humans dependent upon one another. The more we realize our interrelatedness, the more we love. It's inescapable. Yet, sooner or later, all human love is severed and it always hurts. Death is real.

For years, at every funeral, I quoted James Whitcomb Riley's poem, *Away*.

> I cannot say, I will not say that he is dead.
> He's just away. Think of him still as the same,
> I say; he is not dead—he is just away!

I no longer use that poem. It's not true. Those who die are really dead, not just off on a vacation for awhile. They will never again be a part of our life here. In spite of our faith in the hereafter, the separation hurts and we do well to mourn it when it comes.

A young minister went to see Aunt Effie. "She's just grieving herself to death," a parishioner said. "You've got to go out and do something for her."

After listening to Effie's story, the minister decided to take charge. "Effie," he said, "get control of ourself. It's not good for you to mope along so."

Effie responded, "Preacher, I can't help it. When the Lord sends me tribulations, I got to tribulate."

Effie believed in Easter and in its resurrection hope. But Easter comes only after Good Friday. It follows death. Easter interpreted the death of Jesus but did not prevent it. He died. And those who loved Him felt grief and mourned without shame.

Jesus himself wept at the death of His friend Lazarus. If tears were *His* expression of grief, how appropriate they are for us. Those who told us when we were three years old that "big boys don't cry" have done us no favor. On the contrary, *tears are the most effective prayer I know.*

At times, my cry level concerns me. I cry too easily. Sitting in the den with my children, I'll be watching television and suddenly something will touch my empathy nerve. I'll blink my eyes and look away to hide my tears. To me it seems immature and I am embarrassed to cry. Yet, at other times, I'm glad I can cry. I'm glad I'm not made of wood. I feel what others feel. Tears are a common bond among human beings. When others cry, we feel it.

Last winter our church sent a delegation to South America. While there, we had the opportunity to help a family save their home. We gave some money which enabled them to avoid being put out in the streets. When Edward, chairman of our committee, handed an envelope of cash to the forlorn father, emotions were so strong that neither of them could speak. Instead, they both cried. Though neither of them understood the other's language, tears said in a perfect way what they were both feeling. Just so, tears of grief bring sympathetic understanding from the heart of anyone who has ever cried. They feel it with us.

If you belong to a church, the loving support of friends is almost guaranteed. It's nearly impossible for me, as a pastor, to call in a home where there has been a death and not find the women of our church already there. They have brought pies, salads, and baby sitters in an effort to say, "We have felt your tears and when you hurt, we hurt with you."

Someone said, "Misery loves company." Maybe so, and in most churches, misery *gets* company. Loving friends respond to the prayers of those who mourn. A month or more after the funeral, families will gather together and look over the numerous letters and cards received from friends. Without exception, someone will say, "I never knew so many people cared."

Shortly after the death of her father, a teenager said, "Blessed are those who mourn, for they *shall learn just how much they are loved.*" Yet, even more important than the comfort of friends, mourning drives us to God. Often those who are in the deepest grief claim the greatest awareness of God. "All I had to hold on to was God, but that was enough," they say. God's promises become most alive to us when we need them.

A skeptic said to my friend and mentor Carlyle Marney, "I just can't believe the resurrection. I want to, but in this day of modern science, I can't trust in life after death." With great calmness, Marney answered, "Who told you that you have to believe it today?" "What do you mean?" the friend asked. "If I don't have to believe it today, when do I have to believe it?" "On the day you die," Marney said, "or on the day you die with someone else."

Marney was saying that faith becomes real when you need it. If you don't believe now in the miracle of life after death, if you don't know that God Himself is going to carry you to a new and joyous life, *don't fret*. You *will* believe it the day you die or the day you emotionally die with someone else.

I have never doubted the resurrection when it counted. Sometimes, in my study when the lighs are on and I feel very safe, I find myself questioning all this about the dead being raised again.

But I never doubt at funerals. When I stood at the lip of Kate's grave and quoted, "I am the resurrection and the life; He who believes in me, though he die, yet shall he live" (Jn 11:25), and "Your sorrow will turn into joy" (Jn 16:20), I had no doubt.

"And when I go," Jesus says, "and prepare a place for you, I will come again and will take you to myself, that where I am you may be also" (Jn 14:3). I read those words and I cried; not tears of distress, but tears of prayerful faith. When faced with death, I heard the scriptures in a new way. And I believed.

John says, "So you have sorrow now, but I will see you again and your hearts will rejoice, and no one will take your joy from you" (Jn 16:22). Sometimes I cry prayers of gratitude.

So I've come to believe that tears can bring me closer to God. In weeping, I melt away my emotional insulation. Even when I think God is not there, tears heal me. Whether they are tears of anger, or of loss, or of gratitude, I find they have deepened the well of my faith, and eventually I drink from a joyful understanding of God's goodness.

When it's time to mourn, tears articulate my most eloquent prayers.

2
Today
I Can Hardly Wait

"Tom, please believe me. I'm serious. I want you to help me commit suicide."

I had never thought of Joyce as the hysterical type. She shared the success of a professional husband, lived in one of the best sections in town, enjoyed two brilliant children, and sang in the church choir. Joyce was as normal and emotionally healthy as anyone I knew. This talk of suicide baffled me.

"Joyce, I don't know what on earth you're talking about."

"It's Leslie, she said. "I have to go and be with Leslie."

Leslie had died eight years earlier. She had been eleven. Joyce and her family had seemed to adjust fairly well. The necessity of living each new day had forced them to move ahead.

Lately, however, Joyce had become preoccupied with the memory of Leslie's death. She dreamed about her, and fondled those things in the home that Leslie had used.

"You see, she has no one with her. Both of her parents, her sisters, all four grandparents, everyone who knows her is still on this side. Leslie is up there alone waiting for us to come be with her. It's not that I don't like my life here, it's just that it could be twenty more years before any of us . . . well, you know.

"Yes, I'm hearing you now," I said.

"Oh, Tom, I knew you'd understand. That's why I came. I need you to help me. And my familiy will need you to help them

7

afterwards. I know it's unfair to them, but I can't stand the thought of Leslie being alone all those years. If you help me ... "

"Joyce," I interrupted, "I think I can help you, but not in the way you ask." I struggled to say what I had in mind. I had never said it before. I had never even read it. I always feel safer in sharing someone else's ideas. But right then, mine were all I had.

"Joyce, Leslie's not waiting for you to die. She's not sitting up in heaven watching the calendar, biding her time for someone to come join her." I paused then, knowing how these next words would sound to her. I said, *"You're already there!"*

I didn't give her a chance when she tried to interrupt. "You see from Leslie's side, it's all wrapped up. There is no time. I know that's hard for us to grasp. We can't conceive of existence beyond the context of time. Everything we know is related to it. But God isn't bound by such things as space and motion and time. "Remember, the Bible says 'a thousand years in thy sight are but as yesterday' (Ps 90:4). And the word thousand is symbolic. When He says 'the cattle on a thousand hills' (Ps 50:10) are His, He is really saying all the cattle are His. To God, all time is but a moment.

"We see time like a string," I said, "it's stretched out with a beginning, a middle, and an end. We can look back and see where we have been on that string. But God takes that stretched-out string and gathers it up. He rolls it into a tiny infinitesimal ball. And right down in the center of it stands a cross. Clustered around this cross are you and Leslie, and her grandparents and me and my grandchildren. All the children of God, those who have already lived and those who are yet to be, are wrapped around the cross in God's ball of time. He sees us all at once. Time has nothing to do with it."

We, too, can see time wadded up as we look back. Our struggle is in trying to see ahead. From our side of it, we move along the string one tick at a time. But with God and Leslie, the end of the string is already in hand. All time is the same time.

This is the only way I can understand the two judgments. At one place, the Bible says we are judged immediately at death. Yet at another place, judgment comes at the end of the world. I think both of these judgments take place at the same time. When we die, we move from this world of time to God's world where history is already fulfilled. Then those things which seem to us as "yet to be" have already happened in God.

I went on, "You see, Joyce, Leslie is not there alone. You and all yours are already there with her."

I think this is what Jesus meant when He said, "Today." He was dying, to remain in the grave for several days according to our calendar. Yet He said, "Today, you will be with me in paradise."

A unique thing about our faith is the word "today." All religions suggest eternal life sometime. They seek to answer the instinct in us that reaches out for permanence. But Jesus said, "Today," not sometime down the road. It's not a nebulous Rip van Winkle deal with Him. We don't sleep through years of heavenly preparation or wait it out in some purgatory. We don't endure eons of purification nor do we wait for a judgment yet to come. Jesus said, "Today."

Paul says that he "would rather be away from the body and at home with the Lord" (II Cor 5:8). In another place, he writes that his "desire is to depart and be with Christ" (Phil 1:23). Thus, according to Paul, there are only two places to be: here in the body, or there with the Lord.

The Westminster Shorter Catechism asks the question, "What benefits do believers receive from Christ at death?" It answers, "The souls of believers are at their death made perfect in holiness, and do immediately pass into glory." How much easier to accept death because of this word "immediately."

A nine-year-old boy was dying. And he knew it. His mother also knew that it was only a matter of time before he asked her that inevitable question. Then one day he said, "Mother, what's it like to die?"

She struggled to keep her composure. "Remember, she answered, "those late afternoons when you played in the yard until you were so tired? You would come in and after a good supper would lie down on the floor in the den and watch T.V. You didn't mean to, but before you knew it, you dropped off to sleep. While you were asleep, your daddy would pick you up in his strong arms

and carry you into your room. He would gently place you in bed.
The next thing you knew, you would wake up in your own place.
The sun would be shining through your window and everything
was where it ought to be. You were where you belonged . . . in a
bright, new, warm day."

She said, "Son, death is like that. It's like waking up at home in
a bright, new, warm world."

And it all happens "in the twinkling of an eye" (I Cor 15:52).
Today, Jesus says.

I had a professor once who would lean back and chuckle, "We
don't even lose consciousness." But how does he know? Anytime
we talk about the next life we are reading into the unknown. It
can't be proven. Neither can we prove many of the precious things
in life. We can't prove that a Beethoven Symphony is beautiful or
that love exists. Someone has said, "To one who believes, no
argument is necessary; to one who does not believe, no argument
is sufficient." Some things we know without proof or understanding. We don't argue with Beethoven about an eight-tone scale. He
is the master. Nor do we argue with Einstein about math. Likewise,
we have no need to argue with Him who is the Master of such
things as faith. He lived closer to God than anyone we know. And
concerning death, He said, "Today." We simply trust Him.

Mrs. Einstein was once asked if she understood the theory of
relativity. "Of course not," she replied.

"Then how do you know it's true?" they asked.

"Because I know Mr. Einstein."

We may not understand all the things our Lord tells us about
life after death. The symbols may be too much for us. But we can
trust it because we know Him. He faced His own death without
fear and pleads with us, "Do not be afraid" (Mt 28:10). Faith in
Him and His resurrection enables us to die without fear that all is
lost.

Someone asked a six-year-old child as she was hurrying out to
play, "What does Easter mean to you?" She smiled and replied, "It
means the Easter bunny will bring me a basket of candy. I will get a
new dress."

He asked a sixteen-year-old boy, who said, "It means that Christ rose from the dead."

In search of a better answer, he asked a sixty-year-old man. "It means that I have just begun to live."

Many people, both Christian and non-Christian, believe in life after death. We just feel it. We can't explain it. "I just know a part of me lives eternal," a grandmother said. Most of us would agree. We feel a sense of belonging and say our prayers to a Father we know only by faith.

Life after death holds a place in the hearts of all of us, of ivory-palace theologians and semiliterate drifters. God created us in His image and the God within us claims a life with the God above us. The physical body dies. But God's image cannot be destroyed. God made us immortal.

He's at rest now," we hear said as a loved one dies. "The suffering is over and he is with the Lord." When we leave this world by death, we live again in the presence of God. We hear Jesus say, "Today, you will be with me in Paradise," and we feel it.

Two years ago, I met a woman who took Him at His word. Kate had taught school for forty-three years. Four years after retiring, she was dying of cancer. When I visited her, she hardly weighed eighty-five pounds.

Calling on Kate affected me in ways I never expected. I entered the room nervously. What could I say to one who had only a few more days to live? Every hour she grew weaker and soon she would lose her fight for life.

"It's going to be the most exciting adventure of my life," she said. "When I was a child I could hardly wait until I became a teenager. Then, I looked forward to my twenties and graduation and marriage and being on my own. Then the maturity of my thirties, forties and fifties were better still. Each era of my life grew better and better."

Then Kate said, "I have looked forward to every phase of my life with increasing anticipation. But the next life, for me, is the most exciting adventure of them all. Honestly, Tom," she whispered, "I can hardly wait!"

At first, I thought Kate was trying to "psyche" herself up to cope with an overwhelming fear. But the more I listened to her and watched the expressions in her eyes, the better I knew Kate . . . and the more I trusted God.

She believed in Jesus' promise of "Today . . . "

3
You
Everyone is a Special Case

"I wish to God I was not so lonely," my friend Paul said. "Death is terribly personal."

"Everybody has to do his own dying, doesn't he?" I responded. I didn't want to cover up his need to talk about his feelings. I know that feelings don't go away just because they are not expressed.

"Sometimes I feel angry," Paul said. "It's not that I'm that afraid, I've always been an individual, but now I feel so isolated. I wish the experience of dying could be shared."

As I listened to Paul, I hurt with him as he shared his feelings of being cut off from everybody else. But I also realized that God has blessed us in making us individuals.

In a sense, there's no such thing as "humanity," not even when spelled with a capital H. We humans relate to individuals, not to masses of people. We think of Tom, Dick, and Harry, unique people with names, fingerprints, and personalities unlike anyone else. Most of us like it that way and would never choose to give up our unique personhood, even in death.

Often we hear the promise of Jesus from the cross and our minds focus on the first and the last of it. We think of "Today" and "Paradise," the when and where of death. But the words in the middle speak promises equally important. The "you with me" holds all the rest together. These words make it personal. Jesus says, "You." And he means *you*. He is saying that you will be the same person *there* as you are *here*.

Whoever you are, the *you* that lives down inside your consciousness will still be you there. You'll be changed, but you'll still be you. Some would have you believe that the individual you withers and dies like a leaf on a tree. You continue to live only in the tree. A new leaf has replaced you. In the same way, they say that you live through your children, or your influence and memory. The popular quote says, "A man never dies as long as he has friends to remember him." Jesus says "no" to that impersonal life. You'll be more than that. You won't become some oblong blur or mass of spirituality. You won't be lost like a drop in the ocean. You'll still be an individual *you*.

Scientists tell us that our bodies change every seven years. But I am still me. I'm the same *me* I was eight years ago. Changed, but the same me. When I die, I'll still *be*. I just won't be *here*.

A doctor friend said that the greatest testimony he knows to life after death came to him while tending a corpse. "There is a certain negative sacrament evidenced in a corpse," he said. "It's like having a paper notarized." The notary stamps it with a seal. That which makes the impression of the seal is an absence. The indentation comes from what is not there. In the same way, he said, when a patient dies, the lifeless body is a clear impression that the person is not there. The life is free, no longer expressed through flesh and bone.

Flora died. Coming home from the cemetery, her husband, Bob, rode with me. Suddenly he said, "Remember when we went on our trip last winter? We were gone for three weeks. When we got home, it was dark and cold. We drove into the yard. The lights were on in the house. Neighbors were there, the yard was full of cars. Obviously someone planned a party to celebrate our arrival. I drove up, and Flora got out. She walked through the dark and coldness for a moment. Then, she went in."

Bob said, "Just for a moment, the door opened and I could see our friends and children. It was warm and light, fun and laughter. Then the door closed. I was left on the outside. I had things to do. I needed to park the car and gather in the luggage.

So I stayed out in the cold for a while." That's all he said. We drove for five minutes, and nothing else needed to be said. Even though Bob felt Flora's absence, he believed someday he would be where she was.

Then suddenly, he said, "It will only be a little while and the door will open again. This time it will open for me and I'll walk in and join the celebration of reunion inside."

Of course, that raises the question: Will we know one another in heaven and be known? I think so.

Jesus, on the Mount of Transfiguration, recognized Moses and Elijah. They were individuals. He spoke to them. If that's heaven for them, then that'll be heaven for us. "It does not yet appear what we shall be," the Scriptures say, "but we know that when he appears, we shall be like him" (I Jn 3:2). If to know and be known is His privilege, it will be ours, too.

The bigger question than the one about people being known in heaven is, will *I* be known in heaven? I've heard the song, "Lord I want to be in that number when the saints go marching in," but can I be certain that I will be included?

Margaret said, "I have no doubt that all believers are going to be with the Father. It's just that I don't know about me."

I asked, "Are you telling me that you think everybody else is going to be saved and somehow you are going to be left out?"

That's precisely what I fear," she said, crying.

Margaret was dead serious and utterly distressed over her fear of not going to heaven. That was fifteen years ago. Since that time, I have met dozens of Margarets who fear that they are lost.

I once heard of a little boy who prayed, "Our Father, who art in heaven, how do you know my name?" That expresses the amazement of multitudes in our world today. "Among so many," they ask, "how can God possibly know me? And knowing me as I am, how could he possibly care?"

In my own life, I struggle with that same doubt. I deal with it by remembering that God is *love*.

On the cross, Jesus called God "Abba." This intimate way of speaking to God is unparalleled in significance. Abba was the word used by a child calling his daddy. Jesus prayed that His followers might know the Father as He did. "O righteous Father (Abba), the world has not known thee, but I have known thee; and these know that thou hast sent me. I made known to them thy name, and I will make it known, that the love with which thou hast loved me may be in them, and I in them" (Jn 17:25-26). Jesus said that if we want to know what God is like, then just call Him "Father." In fact, just go ahead and call Him "Daddy."

I am a father. And there is nothing my child could ever do that would cause me to put him on the other side of a wall from me forever. If I, then, being evil, as the Scriptures say, "know how to give good gifts to your children, how much more will your Father who is in heaven give good things . . . " (Mt 7:11).

The Scriptures go on to say that "It is not the will of my Father who is in haeaven that one of these little ones should perish" (Mt 18:14). If I understand it right, God cares for me, no matter what. It's not so much that I hold on to God. It's God who holds on to me. He made me and He has a great interest in how I turn out.

My relationship with God grows out of His own heart. What I believe about God, I am privileged to believe because of that relationship. My lifestyle grows out of that relationship. But that relationship does not depend upon what I believe or how I live. It's dependent entirely upon God's love. I am His by grace. I do not believe God will ever let me fall out of His wagon.

Then what about hell?

I don't know! The Bible seems ambiguous about what the word even means. I am convinced that some "hell-fire preachers" have overstated the case. It's hard for me to believe that God wants to force us to love Him by threatening us with an everlasting fire if we don't.

I see a child bringing a flower to his mother. It may be petal-torn, wind-blown, and bug-eaten, but when he says "I brought this to you, Mommie, because I love you," it's beautiful. If, on the other hand, he brings her a bouquet of roses and says "I brought you these because I knew you would punish me forever if I didn't," then where is the love? He acts out of nothing more than self-preservation.

I don't believe God could be satisfied with anything less than our love *freely given*. If He demands our love by threatening us with hell, then it's hardly more than God manipulating us to love Him.

Surely a God of love could not enjoy His home in heaven if *any* of His children were not with Him. Christ came to save the whole world. Paul affirms this when he says, "For as in Adam, all die, so also in Christ shall all be made alive" (I Cor 15:22).

I'm not sure that the Bible supports the idea of an everlasting punishment. Whoever said "everlasting"? The word means "ages," not "forever." According to Leslie Weatherhead, "No words used in the Gospels can legitimately be twisted to mean unending punishment, and indeed, such an expression is self-contradictory. The main motive of punishment surely is to reform the sufferer; in school, to make a better scholar; in State, to make a better citizen. If the *punishment* goes on forever, when does the sufferer benefit by the punishment or use the lesson he has learned so painfully? If hell were endless it would be valueless."[1]

Punishment is never vindictive. The word *kolasis*, translated "punishment" (Mt 25:46), means "pruning," which implies growth or purification but not revenge.[2] God is a Father, not a fiend. A father may correct an erring child but would hardly cut off his love and inflict unending torture.

I wrestle with the idea of hell as torment forever. The most compelling argument against hell grows out of *God is love*. Like a good shepherd, He goes after one lost sheep until He finds it. It's inconceivable to me that our loving Father could ever doom any child of His creation to eternal agony.

"Oh, but God doesn't doom him," said Jim, a young friend one year out of seminary. "Every sinner condemns himself and chooses to go to hell. He could always repent, believe in the price paid by Jesus on the cross, and be saved."

"That's not so," I replied. "You plan is too simplistic. What of those who never hear of the cross?"

"It's our job to tell them."

"But that doesn't answer my question. What about the family living in the next county on the day of Christ's crucifixion? If they

----

1. Leslie Weatherhead, *Christian Agnostic* (Nashville: Abingdon Press, 1965), 286.
2. William Barclay, *A Spiritual Autobiography* (Grand Rapids: William B. Eerdmans, 1975), 60.

all died ten minutes after Jesus cried 'It is finished,' how could they believe in the cross?"

"In that situation, God would treat them as a special case," he said.

"But Jim, there are millions and millions who have no chance to believe."

"Then God has millions of special cases," Jim said.

"Precisely," I said. "In fact, *everyone is a special case with God.*" This includes Margaret and me.

In addition to calling God our Father, the Bible gives us the clear image of God as our shepherd. The good shepherd tends his sheep. He cares for every one. They are all precious to him and if any lamb has special needs, he holds him in his bosom. All night long the shepherd searches for one sheep that is lost. When morning comes, they are all in his fold. He even lays down his life for his sheep.

I believe God loves us like that. A little boy mixed up the words a bit and announced, "The Lord is my shepherd, that's all I want." He proclaimed more grace than he knew.

You are not just a miracle, you are a million miracles. Just think of all that had to happen for you to be here; the dividing of cells, the balance of chemicals, the control of temperature, and the sequence of billions of transactions just for you to be born. The only way to explain your very being is that you come from God. And most of all, God has implanted within you a awareness of Himself.

The stars shine, magnificent, high, and numerous beyond imagination. They extend beyond our ability to see, with no end. Yet, no star ever loved God.

A tree is a miracle, and so is a horse. But even these forms of life have no God-consciousness. You do. Just because you are God's highest creation, you have a certain God-awareness. God invested nothing less than Himself in you.

It makes no sense that God above you would allow the God within you to cease to be. Cecil B. DeMille, the noted film maker, told of watching a water beetle crawl up on his canoe, sink his legs into the soft wood, and die. A few minutes later, he looked again.

The beetle's back split open. A quiver, and suddenly, new life appeared. First a moist head. Then wings. Then appeared a beautiful dragonfly displaying every color in the rainbow. DeMille said, "If God does that for a water beetle, just think what he will do for *me*!"[3]

I read a story that makes this clear. Fire swept through the house. As the family gathered outside, they missed Jon. Without thinking, Dad ran back inside. By the time he found eight-year-old Jon, the front of the house was engulfed in flames. They both pushed back into a corner. Suddenly, a section of the floor fell in and Dad remembered a window in the basement. He jumped down into the dark. Looking up from the basement below he saw his son silhouetted against the flames. "Jump, son," he cried.

"But I can't see you, Dad."

"It's okay, son, I can see you. Jump!"

That's our hope. Not that we can see our way through death, but that God can see us.

"One day, a small crowd will find its way to the cemetery," Kate said. "They will speak quietly and share in a religious ceremony. Then, everyone will return home, or to work. Everyone, that is, but me."

"This earthly life moves toward that for each of us," I said. "We can't see beyond it or any way out of it, so it often frightens."

"That's okay," Kate said, "for God can see me."

"Today, says Jesus, "*you*, with me, in paradise.""

---

3. William E. Smith, "Encounter with Christ," *Pulpit Digest* (March 1980): 69.

4
With Me

The Dark's O.K., If You're Not Alone

"Who wants to go to heaven?" she said, partially laughing. "I've never yet heard a description of heaven that I liked. Gates of pearl and streets of gold have little appeal to me."

"Oh, come on, Kate, you know those kinds of things weren't meant to be taken literally," I said.

"Well, sitting in the bosom of Abraham and singing praises twenty-four hours a day doesn't sound much better."

I couldn't tell just what troubled Kate. The whole idea of dying may have angered her, or she could have legitimate questions about the biblical images of heaven. The Bible doesn't say much about the next life. It uses images. It creates impressions. But it gives very little detail of what heaven is like. This lack of pictures is not because of some careless oversight, but because Jesus approaches us on a totally different plane.

Jesus spoke of heaven in terms of personal trust rather than of physical properties. His promise concerns who will be there, not what it looks like. He describes heaven in terms of relationships, not scenery. Listen to him. "I go to prepare a place for you," He said. "And when I go and prepare a place for you, I will come again and will take you to myself, that *where I am, you may be also* (Jn 14:3).

"That's it," Kate said. "The being with Christ means more to me than all the rest of it put together. I want to be where God is. That would be heaven for me, no matter what else is there."

20

According to the Bible, Heaven is where God is. Hell is where God is not. Jesus promised, "You shall be *with me*."

Death is an existential thing. We do it solo. No one enters that doorway in a crowd. I am certain that one of the great fears of death is that we take that last step alone.

Leslie Weatherhead says that if we had known what this world was like, we would never have been born. Had we known in the prenatal state what a cold and cruel world this was to be, and what condition we were going to be in when we arrived, we would have curled up and never been born. Even before life, we would have been scared to death.

Yet, he says, by the love of God we were not born without a mother. At the moment of birth, just inches away, was all the warmth, nourishment, and love a baby could possibly need. Don't we know that the same God who planned and controlled our birth also has planned for all our needs at death?

"With me," promises that, although we may die alone, immediately, on the other side of death, we are greeted by Him. A little guy walked into church, bowed his head and said, "Jesus, this is Jimmy." When he was sixty years old, he was still doing it. Every time he entered church, he said, "Hello, Jesus, this is Jimmy." One day, a friend asked him why he did it. "Doesn't it seem a bit juvenile?"

"Well," he answered, "I started it when I was six years old. Got into the habit of it, I guess. When I was sixteen, I ducked my head so nobody would see me. But I still said it. Now I'm sixty and it doesn't matter if they do. Every time I come in to worship, I say, 'Hello, Jesus, this is Jimmy.' Soon I'm going to walk through those portals of heaven. Guess I'll feel alone. But then, in that same kind of personal way, He's going to reach out to me and say, "Hello, Jimmy, this is Jesus.'"

Surely, after the resurrection the friends of Jesus must have asked Him a thousand questions. "What's it like to die? Where is heaven?" or "Are people in heaven like they are here? Do they look the same?"

Jesus didn't answer any of them. He gave little information

about life after death. What He did tell them was that they would be with Him.

Death is a mystery and the thought of it frightens even the bravest, at least a little. Jesus knew that information alone was not enough to calm our fears. So, he promised us something far more precious than knowledge about what heaven's like. He said we will be with Him.

I have been with dozens of people when they were dying. *But I have never yet seen anyone die fretfully.*

In the hallway at the hospital, Leroy's family whispered, "It won't be long now. But please be cheerful when you go in. We don't want him to know how sick he is."

Inside, Leroy squeezed my hand. "It won't be long now," he said, "but please don't tell the family. I don't want them to worry."

How much better if Leroy and his family had been free to talk about their grief together. They radiated faith, but more than at any other time in their lives, they needed to affirm it with one another. A week later, Leroy was too weak to talk.

"How do you feel?" I asked. "Are you in any pain?"

He responded by rocking his hand back and forth indicating that he was okay.

Then, I looked into his eyes, "Leroy, are you afraid?"

Again, he lifted his hand and rocked it back and forth . . . and smiled. Three days later he was dead.

Having been with Leroy and dozens of others at the time of death, I have come to believe that God gives to us a certain dying grace. I have seen it. The doctor tells her that the news is bad, it's only a matter of time. At first, she is in shock. Then, she goes through stages of unbelief, anger, and self-pity. But there comes the day soon when she says something like, "I'm really okay. I don't know why, but I feel more at peace now than I have ever been in all my life."

That day long ago in Jerusalem, everybody was afraid but Jesus. Pilate couldn't sleep. The Roman rulers, Hebrew priest, and disciples of Jesus, everyone but the one hanging on the cross trembled in fear. In the midst of it, we hear Jesus declare, "Into thy hands I commend my spirit." He died without fear.

I confess, I'm not sure about me. I keep telling myself that I'm not afraid to die. But I've never really faced it. When the time comes, I trust that God will give me the dying grace that I have seen in so many others. With some of them, it came early. With others, it came only near the end. But with every one, it has always come.

Early one Sunday morning, driving to church, I heard a story on the radio. As I remember, it went like this: Jean sat alone in her apartment preparing for her next day's classes as she had done for more than twenty years. Suddenly, a knock at the door. Unassuming and carefree, she opened it wide. There stood death, hideous and frightening and yellow.

Jean screamed. Slammed the door. She locked it and leaned against it with all her might.

She ran to the doctor. Then there was surgery. And chemotherapy. She went among her friends who said, "Jean, you look wonderful. You have certainly defeated death."

A year and a half later, Jean had almost forgotten. A knock at the door again. She casually opened it, but not quite as wide this time. Again, there stood death.

She slammed it shut and bolted it tight and ran back to the doctor. More surgery, more chemo-therapy. And again she went among her friends who said, "Do you feel as good as you look? You have certainly defeated death this time."

A few months later, Jean heard the knock again. She was frightened but not surprised. She had seen death's shadows hovering in her yard. This time, she tried to slam the door in death's face, but it wouldn't close. The lock wouldn't work and the door no longer fit the frame. She screamed and retreated across the room.

Her friends came. They huddled in front of the door and prayed. "Jean," they said, "we will protect you with our prayers. We will stand between you and death."

I don't know how long this went on, but there came the time when Jean sat up and said, "I'm ready for you to go now."

"But Jean, we must protect you."

"I'm ready for you to go now." So her friends left.

Death knocked down the door and grinned. Jean stared him

in the face. Then death leaned down into his bag to pull out his poisonous darts.

But when death stood up, in one hand he held *rest* and in the other, *peace*. Jean had finally conquered death!

Dying grace is not the result of anything we do. It's God's gift. It's a feeling of certainty that we are not going it alone. We go to be with Him.

Five-year-old Tommy padded his way across the hall in the dark. "Daddy, is that you?" he asked, as he reached out and tugged on his daddy's arm.

"What?" Dad whispered as he strained to see the clock.

"Daddy? Are you going to eat lunch with us tomorrow?"

"What! Son, it's three o'clock in the morning. What difference does it make where I eat lunch? Go to bed!" Dad half shouted.

Tommy drew back and slowly retreated toward the foot of the bed. About that time, a clap of thunder rattled the rafters and Dad caught on. Tommy didn't give a hoot where Daddy ate lunch tomorrow. It was storming now and Tommy was scared. "Son, would you like to leave a light on in your room?"

"Okay," Tommy stammered.

"Or would you like to stay in here and sleep with Mommie and me?"

Pheeaw! Tommy nearly turned Daddy for a flip, he jumped into bed so fast. He snuggled down and fell asleep in two minutes.

When you are frightened, its better to be in the dark with a father who loves you than to be in the best furnished room in the house, alone.

The doctor visited a very ill patient.

"Doctor," the sick man asked. "Am I going to get well?"

The doctor hesitated.

"I don't want to die," the man whispered. "Tell me what's on the other side."

"I wish I could tell you, but I don't know." The doctor squeezed the dying man's hand and turned to leave. As he opened the door, a dog sprang into the house and leaped on the doctor with excitement.

"Did you see that?" the doctor said, turning to the man. "This is my dog. He has never been in this house before. He didn't know what to expect. He only knew his master was here. He jumped in without fear. I can't tell you what's on the other side, but I know the Master waits there . . . and that's enough."

"You shall be with me," Jesus said. "Fear not."

5
Paradise
God Stories Turn Out Right

"Please," the corporal whispered. "... a tomorrow." Early that morning his company of Marines had fought ten times their number of Chinese Communists and had lost.

Leaning over to check his bleeding, a buddy asked, "Can I do anything for you?"

"Give me a tomorrow," he pleaded. "That's all I ask, just give me a tomorrow."

Sooner or later his cry becomes ours, too. We want a certainty that this world is not all there is. No matter how sophisticted we may be, as long as thousands are killed every year in accidents, we are concerned about our tomorrow. In spite of miracle drugs and the wonders of science, the mortality rate is still a hundred percent. Animals may not know that they are going to die, but we humans do. As we recognize our finiteness, we cry, "Give me a tomorrow."

My first week as a student pastor, everything fell apart. Three days on the job, and a member of the church died. Not only had I never conducted a funeral, I had never been to one.

For me, ministry meant trying to gather a big crowd on Sunday morning, fill the Sunday school, and have a fine time at family night suppers. Anything deeper than that and I had nothing to say. I had never seriously thought about funerals.

The church in which I had grown up built a wall around the cemetery. I could forget it was there. Funerals were held in the mortuary. I hardly ever talked about dying. People were said to have "passed on," as though that was less painful than dying. That was forty years ago when death was an unspeakable subject.

My world denied the reality of death. When faced with it, I didn't know what to say. I have not been alone in this.

A young man, newly graduated from seminary, said, "I'm not interested in preaching pie-in-the-sky-by-and-by. I'm interested in the needs of my neighborhood."

"One world at a time," others say. "Why worry about the next world when there is so much to be done in this one?"

Those who feel this way are only half right. Lose the eternal aspect of the Gospel and this world becomes a prisonhouse of hopelessness. Preachers will never mobilize their congregations to clean up the slums until they first give a glimpse of the eternal city of God. Life has its three-score and ten, but beyond this world it continues in the next. Sooner or later, we all have prime interest in those horizons beyond. With fear in our hearts, we cry, "Give me a tomorrow."

For two reasons we dread death. One is the fear of judgment. We fear accountability: that we'll have to stand before God and explain our deeds. Jesus counters this by telling us that judgment has already taken place. We don't have to fear His getting to know us. He has known us all along. We have already been judged, and we have already flunked!

But He took care of that judgment two thousand years ago. "While we were yet sinners, Christ died for us" (Rom 5:8).

Our Lord told us very little about life after death. He gave us no description of what it is going to be like. He anticipated the grave with one word, *paradise*. He returned from the grave with one message. "All hail," or "Rejoice." These words speak a message as much as a greeting. He didn't try to define paradise. He simply proclaimed it. Some things just cannot be put into words.

The Scriptures say, "No eye has seen, nor ear heard, nor the heart of man conceived, what God has prepared for those who love Him" (I Cor 2:9). Some have pointed out that we have no words to describe a sunset to a blind man or the taste of an orange to one who has never experienced it. Jesus simply said, "paradise." It is beyond our understanding.

I can imagine two caterpillars plodding along. One looks up

and sees a butterfly. Pointing it out to the other, he says, "Isn't that beautiful?"

"It sure is," the other caterpillar responds, "but you'll never get me up in one of those things." We are all sometimes like that. God's promises are beyond our expectations. We can't articulate them. So, we mistrust because we can't understand.

A hundred years ago, explorers brought an Eskimo from Iceland back to New York with them. After a visit of a month, the Eskimo went home. A year later, when the explorers returned to the village of their friend, they found that his tongue had been cut out. He had been branded "the liar." It was not within the understanding of ice-oreinted Eskimos to believe the wonders of a New York City. Likewise, there is no way for Jesus to explain to us the meaning of the word *paradise* in terms we can understand.

But hear what the Bible promises:

"I am the resurrection . . . " (Jn 11:25).

"Because I live, you will live also" (Jn 14:19).

"I will never fail you nor forsake you" (Heb 13:5).

Such promises as these are more felt than understood. They are promises of God to *us*. I believe He had us in mind when He made them. When God holds us in His right hand, all the powers of Satan and hell itself cannot pluck us from Him.

A Sunday school teacher was telling in a dramatic way the story of Abraham's attempt to sacrifice Isaac. Suddenly, a little girl jumped up. "Stop!" she said. "I don't want to hear any more." A young friend pulling at the hem of her skirt tugged her down. "Don't be silly," she said. "This is a God-story. It turns out okay in the end."

She is right. And that's the story of our lives, too. A God-story. It always turns out all right in the end. We can count on it. But what of the times we just can't believe it?

After the Easter service, Betty said to me, "Tom, I don't know how to say this, you being a minister and all . . . but I struggle with doubts. Sometimes God seems so far away.

Betty was a religious person. She had gone to church all her life. She had always believed those things Christians were supposed to believe. But, suddenly, she began to call into question some things she had always taken for granted. This was not some suave skepticism which seems fashionable after a year at the university. Betty struggled. She was afraid and embarrassed. She felt as though she were letting God and her friends down. Yet, she continued to go to church. When she thought her family and friends, those closest to her, were beginning to suspect, she decided to talk to me about it. "I just don't believe anymore," she said.

She's not alone. What if we could assemble all those who have struggled through dark hours of doubt? What a crowd that would be. Large enough to include me. You, too. And some would be famous! Some would come right out of the Bible.

There would be the Psalmist, who tells us in glowing language about the majesty and might of God, but who also says, "As for me, my feet had almost stumbled, my steps had well nigh slipped" (Ps 73:2).

Job declares, "Behold, he will slay me . . . yet I will defend my ways to his face" (Job 13:15). Job also cried, "Let the day perish wherein I was born" (Job 3:3).

John the Baptist, who thunders, "Behold, the Lamb of God, who takes away the sin of the world!" (Jn 1:29) also questions, "Are you he who is to come, or shall we look for another?" (Mt 11:3).

Even Jesus, who declares, "I and the Father are one" (Jn 10:30), also cries, "My God, My God, why hast thou forsaken me?" (Mt 27:46).

Stepping outside the Bible, we would have in that crowd of doubters John Knox, who shook his fist in the face of Mary, Queen of Scots because he was certain of God's presence in his life. Yet, we would hear his soul calling God into question.

Martin Luther, whose famous "A mighty fortress is our God, a bulwark never failing" gives strength to the church, also mourned the death of God and often wrestled with doubts.

We would also have to listen to me. And you, too, I'll bet. If you have never doubted, don't brag. Today might be your day. Or if you have never questioned, it may not be a sign of faith supernatural. It may be only a faith superficial. We never question those things that do not matter.

I once argued for hours with friends about faith being able to move a mountain. We wondered if we really could move Caesar's Head in South Carolina closer to Georgia. I changed sides in that debate two or three times. It really didn't matter. None of us really cared about moving Caesar's Head.

But when it comes to the possibility of my prayers influencing a malignancy, then that is another matter. That's when I struggle with doubt. Other people do, too. *Most of our doubts are emotional in origin.*

Thomas had not been in the Upper Room when Jesus showed Himself there. When the others tried to tell him that Jesus was alive, Thomas would not believe. "Unless I see in his hands the print of the nails . . . I will not believe" (Jn 20:25). Now, Thomas was not a skeptic or a die-hard pessimist. He was a disciple. He had followed Jesus, sat at his feet, eaten beside Jesus, and looked up to him. Eventually he put his full trust in Jesus. Then Thomas had seen his hopes crushed on the cross. Thomas' doubt did not come as the result of intellectual debate. His doubt was the product of emotional pain.

Several years ago, we put our son in the hospital. Down the hall was a five-year-old girl who had been born with an open spine. After her surgery, every few hours she had to be turned. In the hallway, I could hear her scream, "Please, Mommie, don't let them touch me!" When they turned her, screams of agony woke up the whole corridor. She shrieked with terror. Then she would whimper for twenty minutes and fall off to sleep. Two hours later, they would wake her up and the process started again.

As I listened to her screams, I found myself saying, "Where in the hell is God?" Doubt grows out of pain.

I find comfort in the father of the demoniac son, who says, "I believe; help my unbelief!" (Mk 9:24). We are not people of faith, nor people of unbelief. We are a mixture. Every believer I know has some doubt. And every doubter I know has some faith.

A member of my church summoned me to go see about her ex-husband. "He's drunk," she said, "and is thrashing about the house with a gun." I went. For two hours I sat talking with him, he sitting on one side of the coffee table and I on the other. A loaded pistol lay between us, the butt toward him and the business end toward me. I agreed with everything he said, as he condemned his wife, and the church, and especially me. We were all hypocrites. Then he started crying.

Finally, he said, "You think that just because I don't go to your phoney church, I don't love God, but you're wrong. I love Him more than you do," he sobbed, "because I need Him more. If I didn't have God, *I wouldn't have anybody in this whole damn world to say good-night to!*"

I learned that night that there are drunk saints. And sick saints and frightened, insecure saints. Faith is always a mixture.

I'm not sure faith is so much what we profess. It's more like what we remember. In the valley, the disciples didn't have enough faith to heal the demoniac son, but they had a memory of the mountaintop.

At one time, I thought that if I just became a Christian, I would always walk in the sunlight, but that's not true. Most of my walk is gray. Sometimes it gets dark and all I have to get me through the tunnel is my memory. I remember those times when I, too, had mountaintop experiences. I have had moments when God was very real to me, when I felt sure that underneath were the everlasting arms. He knew my name and everything was okay. I can't keep those moments. They get away from me. But when I am discouraged, I can remember.

I believe faith is the ability to walk in the dark and remember the sunshine. I believe Jesus knew this when He shared the last supper with His disciples. He knew their lives were going to be painful. So remember, He said, this body is broken for you. My blood, for you. My love, for you. This do in remembrance of me.

Every time I eat the bread and wine, I remember His words. And at that moment it's easier for me to doubt my doubts than to doubt His promises. If you struggle with doubts, if the promise of paradise feels foreign, then I hope you will trust your memory and not your emotions.

John was on the Island of Patmos. The Scriptures say he was "in the spirit" and he had a vision of heaven. John writes that he saw all twelve tribes of Israel. He even names them. They were gathered around the throne of God. The twelve tribes John saw in heaven are the same twelve to whom the promises had been made back in the Old Testament. Not a one was lost. With God, a promise made is a promise kept. Heaven knows, we don't understand how He can keep us when we can't hang on, but we have Jesus' promise, "Today, you, with me . . . paradise."

6
Now
But I'm Not There Yet

"I'm not afraid of dying," Kate said, "I'm more afraid of being sick." She reflected on her mother's lingering illness: over two years in a nursing home, growing weaker and lonelier every day. "I'd rather die today than to let that happen to me."

Kate expressed the fears of every seriously ill person I know. "What do I do now?" she asked. "I believe there's a better life in the hereafter, but what's in the meantime?" That's the hard part—waiting.

I feel sometimes that I have lived most of my life "in the meantime." I've been there long enough to know that if you don't learn to live in the interim, you hardly live at all, Yet, I don't like it. I hate to wait.

I feel as though I'm always waiting for something to happen. I wait for some glimmer of daybreak, for someone to come, or to get well, or simply for someone to call my name. I've spent much of my life in line, waiting for an appointment, or my turn in a doctor's office. But the ill person lives always in the interim, somewhere beyond what used to be and the not yet. So, how do I survive in the interim?

A half a millennium before Christ, a man named Jeremiah lived in the interim. He wrote to the Jews who were in exile in Babylon. They were a long way from that place called home. Their hearts screamed with the memory of those whom they loved and of things that used to be. The sounds of pagan worship baffled their minds. Their hearts were either behind or ahead of them. How could they survive in foreign mud?

When you are caught in the interim, when you are bound and broken down, Jeremiah says, "Build houses and live in them; plant gardens" (Jer 29:5). Jeremiah is saying, when you are caught in an unpleasnat now and have to wait, do the ordinary, next thing. "Build houses and plant gardens."

I have stood by a bed where death has taken a loved one. Suddenly that woman who loved him more than anything else in the world stands up and says, "The dishes need washing. I'll do them before anybody comes." She'll get a broom and sweep the floor.

I remember when George heard the most devastating news a father could hear about his young daughter. He stood in shock for a moment. Then he took me out to his garden and showed me where he had planted radishes and tomatoes. He said, "I think this afternoon, I'll plant some beans."

We survive in the interim by doing the next normal thing. Jeremiah says when you're caught in the meantime, "Take wives and have sons and daughters" (Jer 29:6).

He is saying that if you have little else, you have family and friends. When you can't pay your own way, when you have no strength, when you can't even beg, you still have one another.

When you are forced to wait, seek life where you are. The most enlightening thing Jeremiah said to those caught in foreign lands is that *your* peace depends upon *their* peace. "Seek the welfare of the city where I have sent you into exile, and pray to the Lord on its behalf, for in its welfare you will find your welfare: (Jer 29:7). When captured, put down your roots there. That's the only place you have to live. We can save the flags of yesterday and paint dreams of tomorrow, but we live in the *now*.

The amazing thing is that when Jeremiah's captives sought to live where they were, when they served and sought God there, when they did the next thing and maintained their fellowship and dug in their roots, they learned that *they had been found by God*. He was there, even in Babylon, all the time.

So, we, too, will continue to struggle, to listen and love. We'll maintain the fellowship. We'll hold and touch and kiss. We can be the church to one another, especially when we hurt. We can put down our roots here and seek the welfare of where we are now. We can seek and find God here. The interim brings nothing to an end. It's only one step in a long progression.

Someone said, "That which appears to be an *end* of time is simply an *edge* of time, in which we, too, may discover that we have been found."

"All this talk about heaven and paradise excites me," Kate said, "but I'm not there yet."

"You will be," I said.

"Yes, I know, but right now I'm stuck here. I no longer have the strength I used to have and the promised future is not yet. What do I have now . . . while I wait?"

"Even now," I said, "you have the greatest things of life."

"What's that?"

"You have faith and hope and love." Nothing else really lasts.

"I also have questions, feelings, and expectations."

"Kate," I said, "I think all those emotions flying around inside you are normal."

"I guess so," she replied. "But is it normal for a Christian to worry today about tomorrow? I just don't have enough faith."

"Me, either," I said.

"It's not that I don't believe in God. I've believed in Him all my life. Since I was a child I have been taught that if you put your faith in God, He will take care of you. I grew up singing 'The Lord is my shepherd, I shall not want.' The name of this marvelous benevolent arrangement," she said somewhat sarcastically, "is providence. But I have begun to question providence. Do you think God really knows where I am now?"

"I guess we all picture God as a loving granddaddy, just beyond the farthest cloud," I said.

"I want to yell 'help' and know He'll come running. If He's too busy to come Himself, at least He could send an angel. But can God find me? I'm told that there are stars out there so big you can bore a hole in one and put our entire solar system in it. How in all that vastness does God have time to find little me?"

"I don't know, Kate, but I believe He'll find a way."

Then Kate shifted to her more intimate feelings. "The truth is, I don't want to die," she said. "I don't care what Jesus said about it. Sometimes I'm anxious and troubled."

I understood Kate's fear, and if I had been in her place, I would have felt the same thing. It's easier to preach "Be not anxious" to a room full of people than to face death alone and calm.

When Jesus said, "Be not anxious," He was not telling me that I'll have no troubles if I believe in God. Christianity never claimed to be a peace-of-mind religion. Most of the heroes of the Bible struggled with problems. Someone said, "Adam—had 'em." So did Abraham, Moses, Matthew, Mark, Luke, and John. Troubles, fears, and anxiety are a part of being human. No one escapes them.

I do not control the things that happen to me. Those things the insurance companies label "the acts of God" will sooner or later trip me up. I am limited. I am not God. But I don't have to be God because God is God, and because He is God, I can trust.

When Jesus said, "Be not anxious," he went on to say, "Consider the lilies, how they grow; they neither toil nor spin; yet I tell you, even Solomon in all his glory was not arrayed like one of these" (Lk 12:27). He pointed to a Middle Eastern poppy that grows from a seedling in the springtime, struggles for life all summer, and dies in the fall. Look how God has adorned that flower. "But if God so clothes the grass which is alive in the field today and tomorrow is thrown into the oven, how much more will he clothe you, O men of little faith? And do not seek what you are to eat and what you are to drink, nor be of anxious mind. For all the nations of the world seek these things; and your Father knows that you need them. Instead seek his kingdom, and these things shall be yours as well" (Lk 12:28-31).

No wonder I'm anxious. Most of the time I seek my own kingdom. A part of me continues to live as though I will make it only by my own cleverness. I must take care of myself, for I am the king of my life. But when I seek His kingdom, my life and my health become His problem. No matter what happens to me, He is in it with me.

The Bible said, "Let the day's own trouble be sufficient for that day" (Mt 6:34) Others have said, "Live one day at a time." After all, one day is all we have. Someone said, "Yesterday is a cancelled check, tomorrow is a promissory note. Today is all the cash we have." All we can do with yesterday is commit it to God. God looks at all the garbage we want to drag out of it, the guilts, burdens, and sins, and says "I will forgive their iniquity, and I will remember their sin no more" (Jer 31:34). The best we can do with the past is learn from it and thank God for the memories.

In the same way, tomorrow never comes. As the poster says, "Today is the tomorrow we worried about yesterday."

I find myself waking up at two a.m. worrying about a sermon I have to preach. Then I remember I have to preach one next week, also. That soon grows into forty a year for the next twenty years. That's over eight hundred sermons to worry about in one night. Then I wonder how many phone calls I have to make in a lifetime? I'll bet it's a million. But the great thing about sermons and phone calls is that I only have to do them one at a time.

So it is with life. We don't live it by the lifetime, the year, or even the week. We live it one day at a time, and today is as good a day as any other day.

In the small town where I grew up, nobody ever felt better than "tolerable." That was the common answer.

"How are you today, Mac?"

"Tolerable," he would say.

Only one time do I remember someone who answered, "About as well as common." The code of this attitude declared that nothing today could be very good. The present time was not supposed to offer too much. The good times happened yesterday.

I sometimes get that feeling now. One morning I decided to greet the day like Robert Schuller. I was going to shout, "This is a day the Lord has made, let us rejoice and be glad in it." I said it, smiled, and immediately popped a shoelace. I found a pair of old shoes, wrong color, frayed laces. The whole morning was a flop.

But I had to make the best of it. I couldn't live in yesterday or tomorrow. We all live today.

"But, Tom," Kate asked, "when I'm sick, confined, and uncertain about the future, what can I do to seek the Kingdom?"

"Again, I believe we seek the kingdom by loving God, loving others, and ourselves."

Kate loved God. In her "now," she found time to pray and study the Bible as never before. Kate had limited income, but everytime she put a dollar in the offering plate, she supported the total program ministry of her church. Kate could still show her love for God. Any day she demonstrated that God was her Father was a good day for Kate.

Kate also found others to affirm. She wrote letters she had been putting off, made phone calls, expressed an apology, and recognized important things in other person's lives. "When in trouble, help someone," she would say. In any day, she could show kindness.

But in addition to loving God and others, Kate found time to do some things for herself. Like many of us, Kate had been taught that she was not supposed to love herself. Mental institutions are full of people who still believe that they must live their lives for others at all times. But Kate found time to read a book, watch television, or eat something she especially enjoyed.

In spite of poor health, Kate had many good days. "But I still worry about the end," she said. "I want to be brave, but I don't know how I am going to face it."

I remember Stephen. "Lord, do not hold this sin agianst them" (Acts 7:60). I wonder if I could be so brave. I honestly don't know. I can't program courage. Even Stephen didn't know what he was going to do until the time came, and none of us will, either. Still, I believe we experience an influx of spiritual energy when it's needed.

When I studied science in high school, we were taught a theory of the conservation of energy. According to that theory, energy is always conserved, it never runs down. It transfers to other sources but is never lost.

Now, thirty-five years later, they teach another theory of the conservation of energy. Energy always runs down. It must move from a higher potency to a lower potency for it to be energy. The question is then raised, "Why doesn't the world run down?" Scientists answer by telling us that there is a mysterious influx of new energy into the universe.

I believe that in the same mysterious way, God supplies us with an increased source of spiritual energy. I believed that by the time Kate faced her final moments, she would receive an unprecedented awareness of spiritual strength. If Kate was to pre-imagine the fears, hurts, and disappointment as she approached her own dying, I hoped she would also pre-imagine receiving God's strength with new hopes and peace.

When this day becomes the last day, God will be with us more than at any other day. Waiting in the interim, like the captive Israelites, Kate was found by God.

I trust the message of that beautiful play, *Green Pastures*. The leadership of Moses is transferred to Joshua. Moses stands on the hillside and watches his people go away from him. Everybody he knows and loves walks off and leaves him. Moses sobs. He watches the last one leave. He sits down on a rock with his head in his hands and says, "Lawd, you's still with me, ain't you, Lawd?"

The Lawd walks around behind Moses and puts his hand on Moses' shoulder.

"C'ose I is, Moses. C'ose I is."

7
Faith
Listening for the Right Pitch

One Sunday, a wasp landed on the pulpit. He looked out over the crowd, first this way and then that, paused, stretched his legs, and fluttered his wings. He didn't know where to go. I helped him out. I thumped him over three pews to the wall.

Later I thought: while he crawled around on the pulpit, he had no idea of what was going on. He walked over the symbols sewn into the pulpit hangings. He crawled over gaps, spots, and changes, but he couldn't begin to comprehend them. He heard every word I preached, but there was no way in the world for him to understand it.

We humans are like that wasp. Intellectually, we know little more about God than a wasp knows about worship. For which of us really knows God? We are precious to Him. We enjoy a real, warm, and loving relationship with Him. But we relate always by faith, never by knowledge. When Kate says, "I don't know what God has in store for me," she speaks for all of us. We live by faith.

For instance, it's almost ludicrous to say the word "God" and then try to add anything else. Our effort to define Him simply limits Him. Our descriptions are always unjust.

This was the mood of Carlyle Marney one day when I referred to him as a theologian. He said, "Not only am I not a theologian, there is no such thing as theology. Theology is the study of God. Which of us can claim to know anything about God?"

He went on, "My highest ideals, I believe, are related to God as

He is. I believe I have experienced Him. But when I study my experience of God, I am studying man, not God." Then Marny dropped his voice, "That's anthropology, not theology!"

When we deal with God, it's not a matter of our knowing, but rather what we perceive of Him. It's always a matter of faith.

"Sometimes we can be guilty of practicing theological lust," Marney said. "We claim an intimacy with God that is not yet ours to have. Those local prophets who tell us what God wants and how God reacts claim a knowledge that is not really theirs."

Paul says, "For our knowledge is imperfect" (I Cir 13:9). "For now we see in a mirror dimly, but then face to face. Now I know in part; then I shall understand fully, even as I have been fully understood" (I Cor 13:12). But not yet.

We claim an intimacy that is not rightly ours when we pretend to know now. The promise is future. We have no right to claim it as a "now is." Now we must live by faith. Yet for some, that doesn't seem real enough.

At five o 'clock every afternoon, my youngest son, Jimmy, watches a western on television. One day, he was bored. The program moved too slowly. He said to the cowboy, "Why don't you ride your horse and shoot your gun?" Jimmy is a product of the practical world. "Real" to our world is something done so solid that it takes up space. Nothing is more unpopular than creeds. Someone said, "We want to know what to live *with*, not what to live *for*. We applaud what a man does, not what he professes. Our world evolves around politics, not piety. We move mountains by a number ten bulldozer, not faith."

Yet, every practical thing I do grows out of my faith. I approach a street and stop. I look both ways because I believe if a car hits me, it'll hurt. In the same way, if I believe in the ultimate goodness of man, I'll go the second mile. But, if I believe that you are evil, I won't come close. I'll back off. If I believe that behind this universe there's a God who loves and cares, then I can live the rest of my days unafraid. But if I don't believe that, then I'm an abandoned orphan. And this world is dark, cold, dumb, and damned, and there's no hope. What I believe becomes my fate.

Pop Camp taught me to fly airplanes. He had been flying

almost all of his life. Twice every year, Pop submitted himself to a regulation physical examination which included a chest X-ray.

"Sit down," the doctor said at one examination. "I have bad news for you. Spots in your lungs call for immediate surgery. I will get in touch with a specialist right away."

Pop Camp came home and retreated into a state of depression. "All signs are bad," he told his wife. Our efforts to cheer him up failed. He refused to see anyone and felt too weak to get out of bed.

Two days later, he reported to the specialist, who made his own X-rays. Something did not add up. The original film was faulty. Pop Camp was as healthy as he had ever been. In two minutes' time, his mood changed from sorrow and despair to joy and hope. "Hallelujah," he said, "I'm not going to die after all."

But if Pop Camp had remained depressed after hearing the good news, we would all think of him as foolish. He could have done that. It would have been easy for him to reason that the second doctor was wrong. Pop had to choose whom to believe. Yet, sometimes, what I believe seems so uncertain.

No one has ever proved God. God doesn't even prove God. Ask me, "Is there really a God?" and I'd have to answer honestly, "Apparently not." But God doesn't appear to our senses. He does not demonstrate Himself to our minds. Perceiving God is always a matter of faith.

M.T.

But that's not the same as saying there's no evidence. I am, and always have been, stunned by the mystery of the universe. Some say that science has explained away that mystery, but many scientists are not among those saying it. Some things are too strange.

Every time I see geese flying south for the winter, I wonder, how do they know? The swallows of Capistrano arrive on exactly the same day every year, regardless of the weather. Is it nature, or God?

Some seals migrate over two thousand miles guided only by instinct. Dogs have been known to walk on bloody feet over a thousand miles to get home. Pigeons have been used for years to carry messages because of their unfailing homing instinct. A certain breed of butterfly, weighing about an ounce, makes a long one-way flight from Canada to the Gulf of Mexico.

Some things in our universe can be explained only by incredible coincidence or faith in God. I choose God.

I am told that it would take 250,000 years just to count the atoms on a pinhead. Yet there are stars out there so far away that light moving at 186,000 miles per second would travel more than a billion years to reach us. I'm impressed with the signs of God. I can't explain all that, but I am impressed. I make certain choices when I reckon with the universe. And there are only two options. Accident or order.

I haven't even mentioned such things as goodness and love, which remain the most mysterious elements in the universe. I've made my choice. I believe in God. And just because I believe, I can live in a world that has intelligence behind it, and purpose and meaning to it, and a love within it to hold me up. Of course, some call faith a daydream or a psychological drug. Maybe so. Anything can be turned into burlesque. Even faith is not immune.

Belief in God has always been a split decision. It's never been unanimous. Moses sent spies into Canaan asking, "Can we conquer this land with the help of God?" Two came back and said, "yes." Ten said "no."

Noah built an ark. The crowds laughed. Then it rained, and Noah said, "God." The crowds said "coincidence."

Joshua marched around Jericho. When the city fell, Joshua cried "God." History says "earthquake."

Wise men followed a star to the manger in Bethlehen, proclaiming "God." The community said "hallucination."

At the crucifixion, the soldier whispered, "God." The crowd said, "Thunder."

At the resurrection, Mary cried, "God." Rome cried, "Who moved the body?"

At Pentecost, the disciples cried, "God," and the crowds on the streets said, "These men are drunk."

I guess the ratio has always been about ten to two. And we all have to make our choices. We go as far as we can on reason. Yet, we always reach the place where, in spite of reason, we have to make a leap of faith. Just as Moses stopped and looked at the burning bush, we, too, have burning bush experiences in our lives and we must choose, God or botany.

I choose God. Not because of my understanding, but because in my life I have had moments when I experienced the presence of God.

I once sang Beethoven's Ninth Symphony with the New York Philharmonic. Cellos started the familiar theme which we use for the hymn "Joyful, Joyful, We Adore Thee." Then, violins came in. Then violas, woodwinds, brass, and organ. The music built in tempo, the volume mounted until I was ready to explode.

In that experience—for just a moment—I felt the presence of God. But I lost it. Those moments are never static. I can never freeeze them or keep them. My faith consists mostly of a half-believing memory of those split-second experiences when God seemed real. I look back and choose to believe or not.

I learned years ago while singing in a choir how to listen for the right pitch. In all of life, there are certain things we have to learn to listen for.

Someone explained that fish have fins because there's water. Birds have wings because there's air. Humans have lungs because there's oxygen, and eyes because there's beauty, and arms because we need to hold and be held. *Am I to believe that faith in God is the only universal human experience that does not have some corresponding reality which calls it into being?*

The man asked a little boy whose kite had drifted out of sight, "How do you know your kite is still there?"

"Because I still feel the pull of it," he said.

So it is with God. We move through life aware of His presence simply because there are those moments when we can feel the pull of it.

We can survive in this world without electricity, or indoor plumbing, or clothing, or even fire. We can survive without music or color. We could survive, I guess, without faith in God. But that's all it would be—survival. We could hardly call it living.

Kunta Kinte in *Roots* longed for freedom from slavery. Even death, he declared, would be better than being a slave. Late in the evening he leaned against a tree talking with his friend, Fiddler. "Being a slave just ain't no way to be, Fiddler."

No answer. Fiddler had slumped to the ground and died.

Kunta rocked him in his arms and whispered, "You free, now, Fiddler. Now you know what I been telling you, Fiddler. You free. Ain't free a grand way to be, Fiddler? Just a grand way to be."

All through life, we feel the pull of God to a life that is richer and fuller. Some think of death as the end of the dying process. It's good news, the beginning of living.

I feel that, too. Sometimes. By faith. But I must choose to believe it.

8
Hope

God, Do You Have the Right Number?

"Tom," my doctor friend said, "it's going to be tough. When it comes time to pull the plug, those parents are going to need somebody."

He had asked me to visit a young couple whose five-week-old baby had been pronounced clinically dead. Life-support systems sustained her body, but her brain wave was flat. The State of Georgia requires a second brain wave test after twenty-four hours before officially declaring death and turning off the machines. Leon and Connie were waiting for the second test.

In the next six hours, I did all I could to help them prepare for the next day's ordeal. We talked of the excitement they had felt at their daughter's birth and their hopes for her life. She had come home healthy. Then Sunday afternoon, two days later, high fever, emergency rush to hospital, more fever, and bad news. Now they watched her. She was beautiful in every way, little fists clenched and arms lifted over her shoulders. Except for the tubes, she looked asleep. How do parents accept today the death of their child tomorrow?

That night at home, the doorbell rang. Leon looked at the kitchen clock. 11:06 p.m. "Who in the world, at this hour?" Connie asked.

"We are a group from the St. John's Church," an overweight lady of forty-five announced as she and her friends pushed into the apartment's small living room. "We heard about your little girl and we have come to pray for her."

"Well, that's nice of you," Connie answered trying to get out of the way to make a little more room.

"All nine of us have made a covenant with God," the lady proudly announced. "And we are going to stay here and pray until your baby is well!"

That's—that's so nice of you," was all Connie could think to say.

I began to catch on to what was happening when Connie came back into the kitchen crying. "I can't handle this," she said. "You've got to get those people out of here."

Twenty minutes later, I was still trying to get enough control in the living room to ask that crowd of true believers to leave. "You know the doctors give no hope," I said. "The baby is already dead."

Millie, who seemed to be the group's leader, proudly responded, "What do doctors know about the power of the Lord? As long as there's life, there's hope. If we'll just all believe, God will work another miracle to his glory and we're going to keep on praying until He does.

Then Leon, exhausted at the end of an emotionally draining day, took charge and ordered them to leave. When they refused with remarks about his lack of faith being responsible for his daughter's death, Leon threatened to call the police. Finally they left.

"I'm sorry," Millie said as she was leaving. "We were your hope."

Hope? I thought. That's not hope. That was exhibitionism. They needed to play God so badly that they were willing to force distressed parents to pay the price for it. The price for their trip was guilt so mixed with grief that Connie struggled for the next six months trying to separate them. Not only had she lost her baby, she felt responsible.

"What Millie offered was not hope. It was a neurotic form of escapism," I kept trying to get across to Connie. I remembered once promising the younger Kate that God wouldn't let her husband die if she prayed. I know better now.

It's not easy being human. Accepting our limitations may be the toughest part of it. Sometimes we pretend that we are like God, that we are not limited in power and knowledge. But life has a way of bringing us back to sharp reality. A neurotic says, "Others may suffer and fail and fall prey to disease, but I, by my wisdom or faith, am protected." Yet, sooner or later for all of us, the illusions break down.

Thank God they do. Real hope is a possibility only to those aware of their own frailty. The all-in-control one needs no hope. The world already exists just as he wants it to be.

For this reason, hope has not always been considered a virtue. To some, it's a sign of weakness. "When everything else runs out, when there is no knot at the bottom of the rope, when all gives way, you can always hope," they say.

For years, hope was considered a consolation prize for losers. If you have no resources to face today, you can always hope tomorrow will be better. Mary Martin says, "I'm stuck like a dope with a thing called hope."

Remember the story of Pandora's box. Curiosity lifted the lid and all the evils squirmed out. All except one, the evil called hope.

Hope was an illusion. If you had no power, then you could hope. It was like making a wish.

A little guy goes to the pet shop to buy a dog. The clerk asks, "Which one do you want?" Seeing a puppy with his tail wagging, he says, "I'll take the one with the happy ending."

So would we all. It takes no faith or power to want a happy ending. But that kind of wishing is hardly what the Apostle Peter had in mind when he spoke of a God of hope. He was not talking of a shallow optimism that seeks to escape today's world. Peter was saying that the power of God that claims victory over death is in the here and now. "By His great mercy we have been born anew to a living hope.... " (I Pet 1:3). God's hope has always been given in the midst of life's situations.

The Israelites as slaves in Babylon cried out, "How shall we sing the Lord's song in a foreign land?" (Ps 137:4). They asked for hope. Everything was against them. They had lost it all. They might as well have bowed down and worshipped foreign gods, they thought.

Isaiah spoke to Israel when she was broken and lost. "Comfort, comfort my people, says your God. Speak tenderly to Jerusalem, and cry to her that her warfare is ended, that her iniquity is pardoned" (Is 40:1-2). God comes with a message of hope, even to a rebellious and desperate people.

God's prophets have been prophets of hope. Hosea says that even if you go whoring after other gods, even if you commit fornication, even if you forsake the Lord your God, He comes as a loving husband to buy you back. Hosea proclaimed the hope that is *in God*.

But all prophets are not God's prophets. I remember in seminary days going to a church where I listened to a sermon by a minister of the Gospel, or so they called him. He proclaimed the judgments of God against the evils of the world, namely smoking, drinking, playing cards, and running around with women. As he proclaimed the anger of God against those who smoked, drank, played, and ran around, I felt pretty good. I couldn't afford cigarettes, didn't have time to play cards, alcohol made me sick, and I couldn't get a date. He missed me altogether.

Then he began naming those he had in mind. He called the roll. He said, "When the day of judgment comes, and all these evil people get their just deserts, all I ask of God for the reward for my righteousness is that I may stand at the mouth of hell. As my enemies try to climb up the ladder to escape the flames I want the privilege of putting my foot on the nicotine-stained fingers of evil-doers and pushing them back down into the fire."

Even back in seminary, I knew that was not the message of God. Yet, too often, we hang on to that kind of theological trash. It's still around, even in the church. I hang on to some of it myself, and so do many others.

One day I visited Sharon, who said, "I hate to wake up in the mornings. I hate to start a new day because I know that sometime during this day I'm going to fail God. And that's going to be one more step toward the loss of my soul." As I listened, I recognized the agony she felt.

"Let me give you a gift," I said. "I would take all of that anxiety from you. Your soul is okay; God has already cared for your salvation. He will not give you up. All the powers of Satan and hell itself cannot pluck you from his hands. You can shift your energies from the fears of hell to the joy of your salvation."

She said, "If I could believe that, every day I would wake up singing, and I would love everybody I met. I would be a new creation."

Oh, how I wished she could trust the hope that God gives. He has won victory over sin and death. We don't have to fight that battle. In the first place, we could never win it. In the second place, our hope is that God has won it for us. Give up hope and it's hell for all of us.

In Dante's great classic of the middle ages, *The Inferno*, he gives us a picture of hell as he sees it. Over the door of the main gate leading into hell, he hangs a sign: "Abandon hope, all ye who enter here."

I know of no more frightening description of hell, here on earth or beyond, than a life without hope.

Prisoners of war tell us that enemy guards try to take away every prisoner's hope. If they lose hope, they lose the desire to escape or resist. Their desire to live is destroyed.

The Gospel proclaims that God gives us hope. He never takes it away. How I struggle with that! I feel that when God comes with the good news of His care for me, He must not know me.

I heard of the lady who called a friend on the telephone and asked, "How are you?"

Her friend said, "Oh, I am terrible. My head hurts. My back aches, the kids are driving me bananas, and I don't know what to fix for supper. The house is in a mess and I'm about to go to pieces."

The caller said, "You go to bed right now. I'm coming over. I'm going to take care of your children, wash your dishes, clean your house, and rub your back. I'm going to do your work for you.

I want you to rest."

"Wonderful," the lady said. "I can't believe it."

The caller said, "Tell me, how is Sam?"

"Sam who?"

"Your husband, Sam."

The lady said, "My husband's name is George."

And the caller said, "Oh, I must have the wrong number."

To which the lady weakly asked, *"Are you coming over anyhow?"*

When God comes with a promise of "I will uphold you with my victorious right hand" (Is 4:10), a part of me asks, "Are you sure you have the right number? Is it really for me?"

I ask, why should God love me? Certainly not because of me. It's His nature to love. Out of His heart, He offers the hope and promise of victory over sin and death. It's His victory, not mine. He promises that no matter what, He'll never forsake.

We need that message of hope. Americans spend billions every year for hospitals and drugs trying to combat the problem of depression alone. All of these depressed people are not outside the church. Many sit in my congregation. Many are depressed because of what preachers tell them.

I've preached numerous sermons on faith and love because I have a lot of books on these two subjects. I've never had much to say about hope. Not many people write about hope these days.

One problem with the pulpit today is that we still preach salvation by faith, and not salvation by grace. But when we make salvation a product of our faith, it's just another way of preaching salvation by works. None of us has enough faith to feel safe. No wonder so many church people are depressed.

It's hard for us to get that straight. God comes to us, not according to our works or even our great faith. He comes to us out of His love. It's always a matter of grace. *It's not so much that we hold on to God but that He holds on to us. That's our hope.*

Flagstaff received word from the capital of Maine that in three years' time, a new dam would create a huge lake. It would totally flood the Flagstaff community. Everyone was going to have to move.

Something happened to that town. It came to a halt. People quit painting their houses. And why should they? They quit sending their sons to Boy Scout meetings, and they dropped P.T.A. They quit studying Sunday school lessons and giving to the United Way. The whole town went to pieces.

The Governor sent a deputy to see if some new life could be put back into them. After all, they weren't dead yet. Three days later, the deputy reported back to the Governor. "It's no use," he said. "Where there is no hope for the future, there is no power for today."

I think we have power for today precisely because God gives us hope for tomorrow. We don't have to waste our energy trying to live an illusion. We can quit trying to be God, precisely because *God* is God. So I can say, "Heaven knows, Kate, you don't have to worry. Your hope is in a God who knows."

"Because I live," He said, "you will live also" (Jn 14:19). That's our hope. It's in Him, in the midst of tragedy and death, not in some illusion of escape.

9
Love
But He's My Father

I looked at the casket and all those flowers. Friends send flowers for a funeral service to say something they don't know how to put into words. I struggle with words, too. Every time I conduct a funeral, I seek a better way to say it.

"Martha," I said, "we are going to miss him, too. Of course, not in the same way that you will. Your relationship as Frank's wife was unique, but his memory will always be a part of our church. You see, we loved him, too."

I went on to read those passages of Scripture which promise comfort at a time like this. "The Lord is my Shepherd, I shall not want, He makes..." My voice continued to read but my mind shifted. It's because we loved him that it hurts so much to lose him. If he did not have those qualities that enabled him to be loved, death would not be so bad.

I remember another funeral after Ralph had killed himself. Apparently his love for others and for himself was so weak that he chose death over living a little longer. What a paradox, this business of love. Without it, death is inevitable. Yet the love of God for us is the only thing that can make the thought of death tolerable.

More than anything else, as a pastor, I seek to reaffirm to those facing death that God loves them. This is not always easy to believe. However, we only have to read a little way into the Old Testament to get a feeling of how personal God was to the ancient Hebrew. His God loved, and had feelings. He cared, got angry, and became jealous. Sometimes his God repented of what He had done and did it over because He wished he hadn't done it that way.

All of this distressed the ancient Greeks for whom God was pure reason. Their God had no feelings or emotions. He was the prime being, the unmoved mover. He was absolute. Everything in Him was perfect. He was above and beyond our ways.

In my childhood church, the Greek way of looking at God won out. When the church was forced to crystallize its creeds, Greek philosophy provided the mix. Theologians have been uneasy for centuries about the casual ways we relate to God. They say God doesn't play our little games or get involved in human affairs. God contains Himself within the silence of eternity.

A few years ago some said, "God is dead," or He "eclipsed Himself." If He was present, we couldn't see Him. Others said God "absenced" Himself from the world. No matter how they said it, they meant that God no longer acts on the center stage. He removed Himself from where we do our business. He's not even in the wings prompting. In fact, he left the whole show and we are on our own.

Whether or not we agree with all that intellectually, we identify with it emotionally. Which of us has not cried, "God, I need to know that you are here," only to feel his absence? Sometimes we feel alone and abandoned by God. We reach up to touch the hand of God and we're not sure there's anyone up there to touch us back?

When that happens, we put our logical Greek minds to work and try to make sense of it. We intellectualize. God has forsaken us for a purpose, we say. He let us go in order to test us.

I heard the wife of an alcoholic say, "I have lived in this kind of hell for twenty years because God is trying to teach me humility." Worse still, we sometimes say God forsakes us to punish us.

As long as we suffer in tolerable measure, it's okay to look for reasons. But when suffering becomes unbearable, so intense we can no longer stand it, then it makes no sense to try to find meaning in it. Then we say, "O God, no matter why, help me!"

"Have you ever been there?" Kate asked. "Did you get an answer to 'O God, why?'"

"The only answer I ever get is the mockery of my cry's echo," I said. I find no meaning in suffering and fail to see the wisdom in trying to read the palm of God in every calamity. I don't understand why children get sick and die, or why old folks live alone. I'm like a child trying to understand an adult world.

The doctor enters a child's room, unfolds a cloth kit, puts on the tray those shiny instruments. A little six-year-old looks up with fright, "Oh, Daddy, don't let him do that to me. Daddy, make him stop." I understand why the doctor has to do it but I don't understand why it has to be done.

The more Greek-oriented our thinking, the more committed we are to a God of reason and power. When reason breaks down, we find our faith breaking down. We use God to explain everything from creation to moon walks. But if God is rational, then how do we explain irrational suffering?

At this point, I have to look beyond the Greeks. I choose Isaiah. Isaiah looked over a people who felt they had experienced a full measure of God's wrath. They had taken his judgment on the chin—their land destroyed, their capital burned, the temple in ruins. They had been conquered. The best families were hauled off into slavery, and the rest lived with the nightmare of when it would happen to them. Isaiah said of God, "In all their afflictions he was afflicted" (Is 63:9). God suffers when we suffer.

We have a choice. Many people, like the Greeks, view God as a loveless power. This idea has dominated the thinking of the world. For instance, when the leper came to Jesus for healing, he never questioned God's power. He only questioned Jesus' willingness and compassion. "Lord, if you will," he said, "you can make me clean" (Mt 8:2).

We, too, say, "If God would, he could fix the world." But that's not only Greek'; I think it's pagan.

Years ago Hawaiians looked at volcanos and believed their God had exploded the mountains with the fire of his anger. When it thundered, pagan worshippers went up on the hillside and rubbed their idols. They lashed themselves with whips and cut their arms. Some "chosen" ones laid their children on an altar and burned them alive trying to warm up the will of an angry God, lest His power overwhelm them.

Such efforts to buy God's attention is paganism, but we still

practice it. Many explain Jesus on the cross by saying He was there
to satisfy God, to change God's mind. They say Jesus suffered
agony to wall up the will of God, lest God in His almighty wrath
would destroy us.

Yet, as I understand it, the whole of the Bible teaches us that
we don't have to storm the portals of God to manipulate Him into
loving us. We don't have to tug Him by the sleeve to get His
attention. We don't have to plead, as we so often do, "Oh, God,
please love me. Please hear me, please care."

God loves us no matter what!

I choose to believe that God is love. Most people I know
believe in God's might, and question His love. "Why did God let
this happen?"

I believe in God's love, even when that forces me to question
His might. The God revealed in Jesus was first, last, and always
caring. He was always loving. This truth was so rich for His world
that they crucified Him. They cried, "If you are the Son of God,
come down from the cross" (Mt 27:40). Show us your power and
we'll be convinced. O Savior of the world, if you'll just save your-
self, we'll believe. Let us see your power and we'll know that you
really are God. It never dawned on them that *God chose to show
Himself as God by His love, not His power.*

His disciples often asked Jesus about God. He told them of a
lost coin, and the woman who couldn't get it off her mind. She
swept and swept until she found it.

He told them of a lost sheep, and how it hung so heavy on the
shepherd's heart that he left all the others and searched until he
found the last one and brought it back into the fold.

He told them of a lost boy who had wasted his life. He came to
himself and went home rehearsing his speech. "Oh my father, I
have sinned in your sight. I'm no longer worthy to be called your
son, make me as a servant." As he crossed over the last hill, he saw
someone coming toward him. That someone had been watching
and waiting for him. That someone ran to meet him, hugged and
loved him. Jesus said God is like that someone. Like a father, he
watches for you and comes to meet you. He wants to love you. Add
up Bethlehem and Calvary and we get love, not power.

There are places that power can't go. And things that power

can't conquer. Watching the television program *Roots*, I learned that power can't conquer the heart. That can only be done by love. In the same way, I believe, in the midst of suffering, there are places power can't go. But God's love holds us. He hurts with us. "In all their affliction, he was afflicted."

I haven't answered the question of suffering. If anything, I've made it worse. Now I not only have to worry about why I suffer, I have to worry about why God suffers, too. But I haven't been trying to deal with suffering. I have pointed out that our assurance is God's love. As long as we know that God suffers when we suffer, we cannot see suffering as punishment, as we are so prone to believe. It's a rare thing to visit a person who is ill without hearing, "God must be doing this to me because I failed. God must be getting revenue, paying me back, for my sins."

If God himself suffers with us, it's not punishment. We suffer because we belong to the family of humans. That's the way life is. We have gains that we have not merited and afflictions that we have not deserved. Some things in this life simply go wrong.

But if God suffers with us, it means that we do not suffer *meaninglessly*. When Jesus said, "My Father, if this cannot pass . . . Thy will be done" (Mt 26:42). He knew into whose hands He surrendered Himself. He didn't just give up to some senseless fate. He trusted the eternal plan of His father.

God's suffering with us also means that we do not suffer *alone*. We often see God in human terms. We see Him as a big man. We visualize a hiker kicking over an ant bed. He looks down upon all those disturbed ants running around in circles and he can't tell one from another. They're mixed up. We say God mut be looking down on us in the same way and we're certain we must be lost in all that.

Such a view of God doesn't begin to tell us how big He is. Look how God has worked His plan in just the past six thousand years, and the curtain on the stage of life is just beginning to go up. God is larger than our minds will ever conceive. Yet, in all of that bigness, He gives to us a promise. Nothing happens to you that doesn't also happen to Him. He knows you. He says, "Even the hairs of your head are all numbered" (Mt 10:30).

Paul says, "It is the Spirit himself bearing witness with our spirit that we are children of God, and if children, then heirs, heirs of God and fellow heirs with Christ, provided we suffer with him in order that we may also be glorified with him. I consider that the sufferings of this present time are not worth comparing with the glory that is to be revealed to us" (Rom 8:16-18).

The Good News is not just Calvary. It's Easter. The Good News is not just "I believe in God." It's "I believe in God the *Father*." That's the difference.

William Barclay tells of the little tyke packed in with the crowd on the side of the road, watching the emperor on parade. He pushed forward and tried to break through. A soldier grabbed him and said, "Get back, lad, don't you know that's your emperor?" The little guy said, "Yes, sir, he is your emperor. *But he's my father*." Above all else, God is our Father.

I heard of the father who was pressed into serving as a third-base umpire at a Little League baseball game. His ten-year-old son played on one of the teams. Sitting right behind third was a heckler for the other team.

When the umpire's son came up to bat, the heckler yelled, "Roll the ball to him. He can't hit it." The boy got so upset, he struck out. Next time at bat, the heckler called agian. "Get that girl a dress; he shouldn't be playing against a boy's team." Later, in that inning, he dropped a fly ball.

The boy came to the plate for the third time. "Easy out," the heckler yelled. "Easy out." Just then, the boy got a hit, driving the ball all the way to the wall. He ran past first base, second, slid into third, and was tagged out by a foot.

"Safe!" the father-umpire said.

"Safe? the heckler yelled, running down on the field. "Why, everybody in the stands could tell he was out a mile. Just what kind of umpire are you?"

"Not a very good one, I guess—but I'm one heck of a dad."

I think God loves like that dad.

He is my God, my Creator, my Judge, and my Redeemer. But over all of that, he is my *Father*. He loves me, no matter what.

10
Questions
Why, When, and How?

"Why me?" she asked.

Her friends had expected the question. Wouldn't anyone dying of cancer wonder why?

"If I had done something wrong, I mean something really bad, I could understand this punishment. When I was a little girl and aggravated my brother, Joey, he hit me. I didn't like it, but I knew why he did it. But with this . . . ?"

"I've asked that question a thousand times," her sister said. "It has something to do with the genes."

"I know people get sick for all kinds of reasons. But why me?" Kate asked. "Some people don't deserve to live. Why did God have to choose me?"

Terminally ill people ask a lot of questions, at least inwardly. "Is God doing this to me because I don't deserve better? Why is God punishing me?" Almost invariably those who suffer make a commitment to themselves to "do better" when they get "another chance."

Maybe it's natural to think God operates on some kind of cause and effect basis. We have been told since childhood that we get what we deserve. No wonder we expect life to balance out. We expect the one who trains the hardest to win the race. Thus, when we pull up lame, it's only human to ask, "What did I do to deserve this?"

But to assume that every consequence relates to a moral cause runs contrary to logic. As I write this chapter, I heard of the young mother who was killed while cleaning her kitchen. A cleaning liquid she used to mop the floor ran under the water heater and the heater exploded. She and her two-year-old daughter died instantly. Neighbors rescued another daughter, four years old. Can we explain that one sister deserved to live and the other to die? What about the 127 people who die in a plane crash? Do they all suddenly tilt the guilty scale at the same moment?

I have no doubt that sin produces suffering. But I can't link them together on a one-to-one basis. Kate inevitably asked, "Why me?" and none of us could give a satisfactory answer. The only certainty we have is that her suffering is not a punishment from God.

I believe things happen to us that God would not choose. For some reason, He limits His power, and in spite of all our efforts to make things turn out right, righteous people do suffer. I don't believe that God enjoys pain and anguish. I choose to believe that Kate suffered because, out of the tens of thousands of chances, some of her genes linked up wrong.

To make God's judgment responsible for her illness implies that Kate suffered not only because she was sick but also because she was guilty. If that's so, then Job's friends were right when they told Job he deserved what he got.

"Why?" Kate pleaded. "I know I won't get an answer, but I have to ask. God, why me?"

"No one knows," I said. I reached over and took her hand in mine. Neither of us said anything for a minute or two. When Kate asked, "Why?" she wasn't seeking information. She was seeking understanding. She wanted someone to care.

However, Kate and others who face an imminent death ask some questions for which they do want answers. Kate wanted to know *if she was really dying.*

This question came out subtly at first. "Next week," she said, "I hope some smart doctor discovers a cure for me." Later she remarked, "I don't guess I'll make a hundred after all." Then to her sister she said very casually, "I know I'm dying. I don't care what they say." Kate weighed mostly what was not being said. As her condition steadily worsened over the months, she carefully didn't ask. Then one day, "Doctor, am I going to die?"

"We're doing everything we can for you," he answered.

In spite of his evasiveness, she knew.

Most people, according to Elizabeth Kubler-Ross, noted author of *On Death and Dying*, go through stages of denial, anger, bargaining, depression, and acceptance. I'm sure that's true. Kate did not touch all those bases as far as those closest to her could determine, but she seemed to accept the answer when she asked for it.

At one time Kate expressed anger toward God. "It's just not fair," she screamed.

"I hope you're not blaming God?" her sister said."

"I don't know who I'm blaming," Kate answered.

But I was there and I felt she directed her resentment toward God and I thought it was good. I had no desire to stop her. In fact, I felt regret that during later visits she never expressed her anger again. Anger is inevitable when facing death. Kate had no choice in whether or not to feel it. She could only choose to express or suppress it. I knew she would feel better if someone heard her out. So I listened. Anger, like an abscess, needs to be drained.

On a few occasions, Kate expressed her own needs. Usually when someone asks, "How are you?" dying persons understand that they are expected to say "fine." But Kate found some friends to whom she could say how she really felt, even if it made them uncomfortable.

I think God gives to us a sixth sense with which to recognize those with whom we can share our inner selves. Kate found it therapeutic to risk discovering someone to listen to her. She needed someone to recognize her acceptance of death.

When Kate screamed, "It's just not fair," I knew she had an answer to her first question, "Am I dying?" Her next question was *when?*

No one expects to die young. By all averages, Kate should have lived twenty-three years longer than her grandparetns. But she had a terminal illness and she knew it. "How long?" she asked her doctor. "When will it happen?"

I've never known doctors to answer that question too specifically. They have two reasons to be cautious. First, they don't know. But they would hardly tell her if they did. Kate probably only wanted to know *approximately* when the end would come for her. The anxiety of knowing an approaching deadline can be almost unbearable. Second, Kate herself probably influenced the length of her life as much as medical care.

Curt Richter, a Johns Hopkins psychologist, reports that our attitudes influence not only our manner of death but also its timing. He learned that a rat with hope could normally swim for days. But trim its whiskers and it dies within two to eight minutes. Dr. Richter points out that whiskers are a rat's chief means of contact with the world. Cutting them off causes sufficient stress to create hopelessness.

He also explained that experimental rats were chased into a black bag and grasped by the scientist's hand. Electrodes show that at the moment the rat is trapped, its heart slows down and sometimes stops. However, leave its whiskers and lift it out of the water a few times, and it will swim for two and a half days. All creatures live by hope.

The same principle applies to voodoo victims. The key to their death was that they believed in the curse of voodoo and expected to die. Take away hope, and death soon comes.

I have kept no records, but I have watched people preparing themselves for major surgery. Those who go into it with a positive mental outlook tend to come through it with ease and success. On the other hand, those who have given up hope seldom survive. Many doctors have at least two patients walking around with no medical reason to be alive. Their attitude influences their survival.

"How long will I live?" Kate asked. The answer depended, at least partially, upon how much hope she felt and how she related to life. In turn, the fact that she had some influence on her own fate gave Kate a boost during depressing times.

Kate had still another question. Having accepted the fact that she was dying and having some idea of when, she then asked *how*?

"Does it hurt to die?" she asked.

"Apparently not," I answered.

"I envy anyone who died last year. I don't know what it's going to be like so I wish it were behind me."

According to medical reports, ninety percent of the dying, including cancer patients , can be made comfortable to the end. Patients near death commonly complain of nausea, difficulty in breathing and swallowing, but not pain. Even these distressing conditions can be greatly eased by medical technology. I never saw anyone die in pain.

Yet, none of us really knows what it's like. According to our observation and the Bible's testimony, dying appears to be like falling asleep. It seems the person involved never knows when it happens. The Epicureans had a saying, "Where death is, thou art not." In other words, when our moment of death comes, we will never know it.

"We looked over and suddenly realized that he was gone," family members say. "He just stopped breathing." Like falling asleep. Since childhood, we have linked death and sleep together in our prayers:

> Now I lay me down to sleep,
> I pray the Lord my soul to keep,
> And if I die before I wake,
> I pray the Lord my soul to take.

In the *Book of Acts* we read of Stephen. "And he knelt down and cried with a loud voice, 'Lord, do not hold this sin against them.' And when he had said this, he fell asleep" (Acts 7:60).

Later, Peter writes, "Where is the promise of his coming? For ever since the fathers fell asleep, all things have continued ... " (II Pet 3:4). Over and over, the Bible refers to those who have died as having fallen asleep, certainly not a frightening experience. Calmness, not fear, seems to be the case.

In fact, research, including interviews with thousands of doctors and nurses, often report a sudden rise in the patient's mood shortly before death. It was frequently reported that "they light up, an inexplicable peace and serenity comes over them."

I was present in her hospital room when Annette said, "Momma, I see glory."

Her mother panicked. "Oh, don't say that. You're going to be all right."

"Oh, no, Mother," Annette said. "It's beautiful."

Five minutes later, she died.

I don't know how to explain deathbed visions. Libraries display numerous books on the subject. I mention it here only to say it doesn't appear that the moment of death is a stressful experience.

"I'm just not ready to die," Kate said. "I still have so much I want to do in this life." In the same vein, Victor Hugo wrote:

> For half a century I have been outpouring my volumes of thought in prose and verse, in history, in philosophy, drama, romance, ode, and ballad, yet I appear to myself not to have said a thousandth part of what is within me, and when I am laid in the tomb I shall not reckon that my life is finished.[1]

Everybody dies with unfulfilled hopes. No matter who or how old we are when we die, we leave an unfinished agenda—at least in this world. But it's hard for me to believe that God relates to us only in this world.

Suppose my house caught on fire and I had time to save my favorite coin collection or my child. Is there any question about which I would save? Is God any less? Would He keep the hobby and let his children go? The Bible tells us that we are the crown of His creation, made in His image, more marvelous than all the planets.

The children in our church sang an anthem which declares the bigness and beauty of the stars. But, they sing, I am greater, for the stars in all their glory cannot say "Good night to God." As they sang, I thought of Kate.

She lived, but the stars are dead.

---

1. Quote from Charles F. Hoone, "Daybreak Over an Empty Tomb," *Pulpit Digest* (March 1981):63.

She thought but they don't know they're even thought about.
She loved, but they have no emotions.

She developed faith, but the stars do not even meditate.

Kate worshiped, loved, and contemplated a life to come. Would God save the dust and leave the spirit to die? Would he keep the lowest and let the highest go?

Jesus said not. "When I go and prepare a place for you, I will come again and will take you to myself, that where I am you may be also" (Jn 14:3).

Paul said, "No eye has seen, nor ear heard, nor the heart of man conceived, what God has prepared for those who love him" (I Cor 2:9).

Worlds come and go, but the promises of God remain. I remember hearing of a hot summer night in Mississippi. Meteors flashed through the sky in a frightening way. Slaves on the row ran and cried, thinking the stars were falling as a judgment. A crowd gathered around the cabin of ol' Mose.

"Mose, ain't you afraid?" they asked.

"Naw," said Mose. "I ain't scared. Look at them big stars. They still shining and they ain't moved an inch."

So it is with us. This earthly life flashes for a while and falls. But the big life, the one held in the promises of God, still shines. "It ain't moved an inch."

Kate asked why and when and how. The only answers she found gave her very little information. But what she really wanted was to be reassured that God had some answers and that she was His.

11
Feelings
Earth is a Lonely Place

"I'm no good for anyone anymore," Kate said. "I can't even take care of myself."

I didn't know what to say. I just listened.

"I'm miserable. Even among my friends, I feel lonely. Paul said faith, hope, and love abide, and the greatest of these is love. But I also experience the opposite. I struggle with doubt, death, and loneliness. And the worst of these is loneliness."

I should have expected Kate's loneliness. She reminded me of a *Peanuts* cartoon in which Linus stood in front of the library, afraid to go in.

"Why are you afraid of the library?" Charlie Brown asked.

"It's such a lonely place," Linus answered.

"Why, everybody has some place to be lonely."

"Where is your lonely place?" Linus asked.

"Earth," Charlie Brown answered.

We all understand him. Earth is a lonely place.

"All of man's history," says psychologist Rollo May, "is an endeavor to shatter his loneliness." Everyone falls victim to it sooner or later. We begin life alone, locked up in our own space of being, thinking, and feeling. Loneliness is built in. We spend most of our life trying to overcome it. Yet, we seldom do.

We change the place and the name of it, but we never escape it. We get busy, or rich, or angry, or well known. We even lead the crowd in an effort to attract others to us, but loneliness still writes itself across the lines of life. We may sing with Billy in *Carousel*, "You'll never walk alone." But the words lie on our lips, for we do walk alone. In spite of all our modern advances, rockets to the moon, and mechanical hearts, we still don't know how to conquer our loneliness. Earth is a lonely place.

From the moment we are born, we reach out for others. We humans spend more time with our families and parents than any other animal creature. Strong, loving hands hold us at birth. They lift us and we remember the closeness of a mother's warm body. Psychologists tell us that we constantly seek to recapture those first warm and nourishing feelings. Without them, we become hostile and angry at the whole world. But we never make it. We live the significant feelings of life—birth, fear, hope, faith, and death— alone.

Someone said that we sit in our homes surrounded by our fences, yearning to have some contact with other people sitting in homes surrounded by their fences. Teenagers wear the same kind of blue jeans to be a part of the in-crowd.

"Each of us is lonely," Ann Landers said. "We cry to be understood because we are frightened and confused inside. Yet we wear a mask."

Some consider loneliness a weakness. "I'm too strong to be lonely," they say. Yet many of those so-called strong people have just been smart enough to find ways to cover up their loneliness. Some hide from it in their work while others camouflage it in religion. But sooner or later, regardless of age or strength, each of us feels lonely.

Kate, because of her age and health, felt a special kind of loneliness. Our society has an aversion for dying people. They are often abandoned. They represent a minority group who make us uncomfortable.

Kate's family, suffering from a misguided compassion, pretended that nothing frightening would ever happen that Kate could not handle. They assumed that Kate either didn't know the worst or chose not to talk about it.

I don't suggest that anyone rush in and say, "Okay, Nannie, you're dying. Let's talk about it." But those who love her can be sensitive to Nannie's questions and feelings. On the other hand, those who control the direction of the conversation even before it begins treat Nannie like a non-person. Like everyone else, Nannie is a living being with a past and a future. She has interests, concerns, and a viewpoint. She needs someone to listen to her.

If Nannie represents most terminally ill patients, her greatest fears are not of physical pain but of being abandoned. She fears being put in an institution such as a nursing home. That probably won't happen. I admit that when I think of aging people, I ususaly picture an institution for shut-ins, but I'm wrong. If my congregation represents an average, ninety-five percent of those over sixty-five are not in institutions. They live in their own homes or apartments. Four out of five get out and around on their own. Most are not considered "meddlesome old fools," or "in the way," as some people picture them.

But they are often treated as such. I remember visiting a family in which a seventy-nine-year-old grandmother lived. The family assumed she was senile so they treated her like a child. They spoke baby talk to her, often in the third person as though she were not present.

"We wove you but it's time now for Nannie to go nighty-night," her daughter said.

"Hold out your little hand now," a child said, "and I'll give you a little surprise."

"But I don't care for squash," Nannie said.

"Clean your plate, dear, or you don't get any dessert. Remember what the doctor said."

Another way to contribute to Nannie's feelings of isolation is to withhold family concerns from her. Last month, one of the children had a medical problem. The family decided to spare Nannie the worry and not tell her. Later, after the operation, when Nannie found out, she said, "Why didn't you tell me?"

Nothing they said helped Nannie to feel like part of the family. She no longer felt important or needed, not even to share family concerns. Loneliness comes to everyone, but especially to the aging.

Chaplain Joseph Rowan of the Walter Reed Army Hospital

tells of visiting an old general. Rowan read the words of Jesus to Peter: "I tell you most solemnly, when you were young, you put on your own belt and walked where you liked; but when you grow old you will stretch out your hands, and somebody else will put a belt around you and take you where you do not wish to go" (Jn 21:18, Jerusalem Bible).

> These words could have been written over the door of the old General's room. As I entered, the General was sitting, shoulders stooped, blue-veined hands folded, and eyes staring in disgust and utter defeat. There was blood all over the walls, the bed, and the General. He kept forgetting the intravenous tube and pulled it out every five or ten minutes, causing rage, shame, frustration, and a lot of bloodletting. The object of his baleful rage was a shining silver bedpan.
>
> The General was once a brilliant football star at the Military Academy, the commander of an infantry division in combat and a corps in Korea, and had served on MacArthur's staff in the Far East Command. He had proudly worn three stars on his shoulders. That bedpan was a symbolic blot on a proud and gallant shield. The General was 82 years old.
>
> The charging legs that had churned across the goal lines of yesterday were tethered to an area the length of a thin piece of tubing. Eyes that pored over maps and battle plans were dull and staring. The voice that moved battalions and regiments and put fear in the hearts of staff was cracked and muttered malevolently, 'That god-damned bedpan!' Somebody else put a belt around him and took him where he did not wish to go.[1]

Age and illness threaten us all if we are strong enough to live that long. But in the latter time of life, we all, without exception, lose our strength. The crisis of old age weighs heavy enough on us; we deserve the support of those who love us, never their ridicule or condemnation.

I read of the grandfather, father, and son who were eating together. Grandfather accidently broke his plate.

"You careless ol' fool," the father said. "Just for that, you'll have to eat out of a wooden bowl."

---

1. *Pulpit Digest* (May/June 1977): 8.

Later, the father came upon the son carving on a piece of wood. "What are you doing?"

"Making a bowl, the son said, "for you when you are old."

Earth is a lonely place, especially for the aged, and we all have our turn.

Kate was fortunate in having a family to support her during her latter years. But there are several things Kate did for herself.

Kate used this time to draw closer to God. She realized that loneliness is God-given.

The inevitable loneliness of life is a natural expression of the fact that we are individuals. Each of us lives alone, makes personal decisions, and feels our own private emotions. This affirms our own special worth; so special, someone said, "that no one else can do our living for us, unless we choose to let them."

There are two ways Kate could have dealt with loneliness. She could have looked at it as an unfortunate condition. She could have given herself to watching T.V., playing cards or visiting her hairdresser to keep herself occupied. She might have lost all interest in life except memory of the past and her fantasy. She could have lived her every moment in fear.

But Kate chose to see her loneliness as an opportunity. God did not make us this way by accident. We need private experiences. Jesus suggested that we go into our closet and shut the door and pray. Often it's when we are alone that God becomes most real to us.

Kate had a valuable opportunity to spend time in meditation. There is a part of life that cannot be shared by another person. We have an inner awareness that can be touched by God alone. Human relationships cannot fully answer our feeling of separation. Some describe it as a hunger. "As a hart longs for flowing streams, so longs my soul for thee, O God" (Ps 42:1) expresses the sense of incompleteness we humans experience.

We may try substitutions: absorption in career, entertainment, or even religious activity, but nothing can fill our deepest loneliness but God Himself. Kate overcame the emotional trauma of loneliness when she used her solitude to draw nearer to God. In reality, loneliness can be God's way of drawing us out of ourselves to make us more aware of Him. Kate also used this time for intercessory prayer.

I saw her one day marking up the newspaper. She circled stories. First, one about a trucker killed on the highway, then a family burned out, and then a runaway teenager. She finally circled the obituary column.

"What are you doing?" I asked.

"I read the paper to become aware of people who have trouble. Then," she said, "I pray for those who don't have time to pray for themselves." She also spent extra time praying for those she loved on birthdays, anniversaries, and other special days.

Kate worshiped in her church. Her hour on Sunday morning with friends became the high moment of her life. To most people, church was an option, but Kate needed to be there to meet a group of friends who missed her when she was not there.

She was like the lady who visited the Post Office. "Look," the postman said, "we have new machines. From now on, you can buy your stamps out of the machine and not have to stand in line. Isn't that wonderful?" he said.

"Yes, I guess so," the lady answered. "But will it ask me about my rheumatism?" Kate needed friends to ask her about her rheumatism. Church gave her a place to belong and be cared for.

Another thing I noticed in Kate was her willingness to risk. Some poeople are lonely because they are afraid to approach people on a deeper level than a superficial one. They fear rejection. But Kate trusted her sixth sense to tell her with whom she could safely share her inner self. When she expressed her loneliness, she became real to another person.

"Anyone can share my smiles," she said, "but only a special friend can share my pain." Kate risked being vulnerable with a few close friends who talked about their needs and suffering without embarrassment.

On some days, she made phone calls to others she thought might also be lonely. She wrote letters to keep in touch. Some people buy cosmetics or a new wig. Kate used her time to strengthen her relationships with God and her friends.

Kate took upon herself a project to heal any broken relationships, as she said, "to fogive my debts as I have been forgiven. When you are waiting to die, it's time to be honest."

I heard of the four-year-old who prayed, "Forgive us our trashbaskets as we forgive those who put trash in our baskets." Many people had put trash in Kate's basket. They had hurt her, let her down, and deserted her when she needed them. Kate had cause to be angry. In times past, like most of us, she had looked for ways to retaliate against those who had mistreated her. Now, Kate had time to analyze the hurts and be honest about blame.

"I remember as a child often fighting with my brother. When Mother would walk in and make us stop, I always explained, 'It's Joey's fault,' I'd say, 'He hit me first.'

"I'm sure, at the time, I believed he did. Now, I know me well enough to know that the fault couldn't have always been his," Kate said. She accepted her own part in broken relationships and was able to forgive herself and others.

The Gospel doesn't say that if you're innocent enough, God will forgive the rest. God recognizes that we are not perfect. But He loves us good and bad, warts, wrinkles, and all. Just as God has forgiven us, He wants us to forgive one another.

I don't know anything more important for emotional strength than to accept and often declare forgiveness. In doing so, Kate honored God's love and emptied her basket of yesterday's trash.

"Some days feel like a new birth," Kate said, "rather than dying times."

Still, sometimes, no matter what she did, she felt sad. But nowhere does it say that a Christian must be happy and chipper all the time. Kate was only human, and sometimes the shadow got long in the valley. Like Elijah, she felt "it is enough, Lord, now take away my life."

The Lord sent angels to minister to Elijah. The promise of the Gospel is not that Kate would escape loneliness, but that God would be with her in the midst of it.

"What are you going to be when you grow up, Charlie Brown?"

"Lonely," he said.
Kate understood, I believe.

12
Expectations
Growing, Glowing, and
Hurrah for Jehovah

"Are you afraid to die?" Kate asked. "I mean, what do you think it's going to be like?"

"I used to be afraid, as a child," I said. "But now, I don't know."

Somewhere between the ages of five and ten, I realized that death ended every life. Mine, too. No one else seemed disturbed about it, so I kept my fears to myself. I heard predestination-damnation sermons that assured me that, except for the elect, death was everlastingly horrible. I hoped I was elect, but I wondered. I belonged to the church, said my prayers, and did all the things I was told a Christian should do, but the thought of dying still frightened me. Death, it seemed, was God's way of getting even with bad people.

I remember a classmate who fell into a logging saw. Suddenly, everyone talked about how horrible to be snuffed out at fourteen. The next Sunday, though, our minister assured us that "this beautiful child of God now experiences the ecstasies of heaven." But I knew that particular child of God and he often had resembled those whom our preacher had described in his sermons as hell-bound sinners. I was confused and frightened. Most of all, I felt relieved that death had taken him and not me.

Now, almost forty yers later, I think I'm not quite as afraid of death. But I'm not ready for it. One night last year, I awoke at three a.m. My heart pounded and I felt pain in my chest. I tried to sit up but couldn't. This is it, I thought. From that moment on, everything I did was irrational. I didn't call for help. I didn't pray. I broke out in a sweat and waited to be kicked in the chest by a mule. I knew I was having a heart attack and I was immobilized with fright.

As it turned out, I was fine, nothing wrong with my heart. I don't know what happened to bring all that about, maybe a dream.

"But, you believe in life after death, don't you?"

"Yes," I said, "but I have mixed feelings. What happens after death causes me no problems. It's dying that makes me anxious."

I believe in eternity. It's almost impossible not to. Death *looks* final but I have learned not to judge anything by its appearance. An unseen world surrounds me every day.

For instance, this book looks solid. But scientists tell us that these pages are a group of whirling atoms, anything but solid. Everything I see, they say, is a moving shield of an unseen world. The room in which I sit is full of music. I just can't hear it without a radio, and it is full of pictures I can't see without a television. I can't see love or touch guilt but I know when it's present. There is a whole world of unseen realities that make up the strongest influences on my life.

Eternity is not something that I will encounter at death, but I am experiencing eternity right now. John said we have already "passed from death to life" (Jn 5:24). That part of me believes in life after death.

Nature also influences me. The sun goes down and apparently dies. Yet every day brings a new dawn. The plant dies and from its seed blossoms a new flower. Spring follows every fall.

I remember reading of an old building near London torn down to make room for a highway. The ground that had once been covered by the building suddenly began to produce flowers. Botanists from all over England came to examine this strange growth. They finally determined that the flowers sprang from seeds scattered by the Romans almost two thousand years earlier. I believe in life after death.

I can't believe the talent of Leonardo da Vinci, the genius of Ludwig von Beethoven, and the faith of Martin Luther died with the body. I refuse to think that the crown of God's creation can be wiped out forever by a microbe or a drunken driver. I believe we were created for more than this life.

I remember affirming this in a sermon. I told of the old trapper who came to the trading post when his supplies ran out. As he walked up on the porch, he noticed an eagle in a cage. During the next hour, he traded furs and money for food, blankets, and rifle bullets. Then he said, "How much you want for that eagle?"

"Ten dollars," the proprietor answered, "for the bird and the cage."

"Deal," said the trapper. He loaded up his donkey and picked up the eagle's cage. Taking his knife, he pried open the door. The eagle hesitated for a moment, sprang from its feet and gracefully flew away.

"Go, boy," the trapper said. "You weren't meant for no cage. Your kind was made for the skies."

In the same way, this earthly life reaches the place where it cages us. Death is like God's setting us free. I believe that we, too, were made for the skies.

I believe it, yet a part of me remains unsatisfied. In my experience, the eagle is not released; the eagle always dies. I believe God raises him up to new skies, but first, he dies in the cage.

"This is the point where I am most dependent upon God," I said to Kate. "But I used to be more than I am now. When I was younger, I imagined myself dying at the age of 102 with my boots on, fully active and in control. But the older I get, the more my fear turns to excitement."

"Excitement?" Kate said. "You feel excitement? Just what do you expect of life after death?

"I'm no expert, Kate. When it comes to death, we're all amateurs. But I will share, as one friend to another, what I believe about the next life."

And what do I expect?

First, I expect the next life to make sense out of this one. I look around this world and things seem to be out of balance. One person enjoys good helath while another suffers and dies in the prime of life.

For instance, there were two brothers in my congregation. Hal graduated from high school with honors. He possessed a winsome personality and was preparing to enter medical school. Pat, the younger brother, was retarded. His life was filled with frustration and pain. The financial and emotional burden on his family at times seemed almost unbearable.

One night while driving to visit a friend, Hal and Pat were hit by a drunken driver. The accident killed Hal and left Pat uninjured.

Bad things happen in this world that never make sense if there's no life beyond. Somewhere, a loving God must make things right. Heaven is a place of reunion.

When someone I love dies, I miss him. I miss his voice, friendship, and personality. If he were simply visiting his family in another town, I would feel differently about his absence. I would picture him laughing and working in his own home. I could also look forward to the time when he would come back and share life with me again.

I expect the next life to be a time when I greet old friends who have gone before me. But, more than that, I expect heaven to be as John described it. "God himself will be with them; he will wipe away every tear from their eyes, and death shall be no more, neither shall there be mourning nor crying nor pain any more, for the former things have passed away" (Rev 21:3-4). I think this means Pat will be smart and Kate will be young and healthy. All the wrongs of this world will be corrected.

When John saw "a new heaven and a new earth," he proclaimed, "the sea was no more" (Rev 21:1). We often think of the sea as a choice place of rest. But to the ancients, the sea represented everything dangerous, every pain, fear, or sadness. John looked into heaven and said, "Hallelujah! Hallelujah! For the Lord our God the Almighty reigns" (Rev 19:6).

"What do I expect in the next life?" I responded to Kate, "I expect God to make everything right. Hallelujah!"

Second, I expect heaven to be a place of exciting growth. If there's life, there must be challenge and expression.

I remember the story of the man who died. Early the next morning he woke up to a beautiful world and a room full of servants. Everything he wanted was at his fingertips. He snapped his fingers and servants fed him steak and lobster. They laughed at all of his jokes. He won every game of solitaire and knew the answer to every question.

When he played golf, each shot was a hole in one. This unfailing success went on day after day. Finally he asked his servant if things could be changed. He would like to miss just one putt.

"I'm sorry," the servant said. "But that's the one wish I cannot grant you."

"If this is the way things are going to be," the man said, "I'd just as soon be in hell."

"Sir," the servant said, "Just where do you think you are?"

I can't think of a worse fate than to have completely arrived in every aspect of life. Surely there will be opportunity for continued growth in heaven. In this life, I am just beginnning to learn to love and have faith. Will my growth be wiped out or no longer relevant because my physical life ends?

But toward what will we grow? I think we'll grow toward a more perfect relationship with God. Heaven has less to do with the length of time than the quality of it. We begin that relationship here. John says, "He who hears my word and believes him who sent me, has eternal life" (Jn 5:24).

I will continue to grow there in a relationship with God which begins here. God will give me the power to become all that He created me to be.

I think of the children's sermon told by David Fry, my colleague in ministry, about the experience of a light bulb. This light bulb sat on the grocery store shelf, packed in tight among its friends. One day a customer walked by, reached up, and snatched it off the shelf.

"Oh, no," the bulb said, "What's happening to me now? Put

me back; I'm scared." But the bulb was dropped into the bottom of a shopping cart, covered up with more than a dozen grocery items.

Then it was thrown into a large paper bag and carried off to a strange house. For months the lonely light bulb lay on a closet shelf in the dark. What a sad, meaningless life, the bulb thought. I wish I were back in the store with my friends.

Then the closet door opened. A hand reached in and picked up the light bulb. "No," yelled the bulb, "they're stripping off my jacket. What's going on? They are screwing me into a socket and hanging me by my feet from the ceiling. What's she doing now?" the bulb asked as the lady walked over and flipped the wall switch.

"Wow!" the bulb yelled. "Whee. Look at me. I'm glowing, I fill the whole room with light. Now I know why I was made. Boy, I wish those bulbs back at the store could see me now. Hallelujah!"

I think God has that kind of experience in store for me, and Hal and Kate.

Kate celebrated her seventy-first birthday in the hospital. She hardly knew it. Large doses of morphine kept her groggy, barely free of pain and constantly nauseated. Her time was near.

"She doesn't have a chance," her sister, Emily, said. "You know they removed most of her stomach trying to get the tumor. Now this blood clot in her lungs means more surgery. All this on top of her heart problem. She's not going to make it this time."

"Are you sure she wants to?" I asked.

"No, she doesn't want to. She told the doctors not to keep her alive on a machine. Her life, at times, was unbearable."

Three days later, Kate was conscious enough to ask if "special procedures" had been used to prolong her life.

"We did what was necessary," the doctor answered. Kate's heart had stopped. The cardiac arrest team revived her—four times.

"Why would you do it?" Kate asked, barely loud enough to be heard.

One more decision, Kate," I said.

"What now?" she asked.

"*Where?*" I responded. "You have to decide where to die."

"I want to be near my family if I can," she said.

Kate just dropped off in her sleep less than six weeks after her last surgery. But she had made the kind of decisions that brought her dignity and self-worth in the process of it. "Heaven knows," she said. "I'm trying to make the best of all this."

As I watched Kate give of herself even as her life was being slowly crushed by age and disease, I thought of a strange phenomenon. A flower leaves its fragrance even on the sole of the foot that crushes it. Kate did, too.

Kate died before this book was finished, and I conducted her funeral. The last word I spoke at her sevice was "Hallelujah!" It means "Hurrah for Jehovah!"

I don't know, of course. But I believe Kate's first word in heaven must have been:

"Hallelujah!"

"Be there!"

13
Secret
Look Up

It rained as I boarded the plane. We taxied to the runway through fog and night-like darkness. What a dreary day, I thought.

Ten minutes after taking off, we broke through the clouds. The sun shone from a blue sky and brightened up the white cloud puffs below. We flew for an hour through the most beautiful day I could imagine. Then we sank back down into the dark clouds to land in rain and fog again. I looked at the crowd of people rushing through the gloomy day and felt as though I knew a secret. Hey, folks, I wanted so say, above all this it's beautiful!

I think Jesus had in mind the active will of God for this world when He spoke to the crowds in Jerusalem. "Now when these things begin to take place, look up and raise our heads, because your redemption is drawing near" (Lk 21:28).

Through all His life, Jesus claimed a present nearness of things above. We do not see the whole picture by looking around us.

Around us we see a catalogue of calamity, suffering, and death. We ask *why* and no one answers. Some say it's because of our sin. Or worse, they say it's because God sleeps at the switch. But most of us just don't say. We have no answers.

Jesus never answers *why*. But He does say *what*. In the midst of calamity, look up! For God draws near. When troubled the most, I become most aware of God. I am convinced that more serious

God-thought takes place in hospital rooms than in the average church pew.

When the world seems to come to pieces, I need to be reassured that God made it and that it's God's world. In the same way, when I hurt, I need to be reminded that I'm also God's *me*. He made and values me.

I heard about a profound experience which took place at a Billy Graham campaign. Ethel Waters sang the hymn, "He's Got the Whole World in His Hands." When she had finished singing, the crowd sat hushed. She then leaned into the mike and whispered, "He loves ya', honey, because He made ya'."

Then she walked away, about six feet from the mike. People in the front rows said they heard her grunt, "Hmmp," and she walked back. "You can believe it, honey, God don't make no junk!"

Several weeks after the kidnapping of Reg Murphy, editor of the *Atlanta Constitution*, I led a small group which met once a week in my office. I had a poster which read GOD DON'T MAKE NO JUNK on my wall. One of my friends pointed to it and asked, "What does that mean ... that Reg Murphy is not junk and shouldn't be hauled around in the trunk of a car like a spare tire?"

"Of course, that's what it means," I said. "But it also means that William Williams, the one who kidnapped him, is not junk. He acted junky when he didn't know who he was. For some reason, he thought he had to do something spectacular to make himself somebody."

William Williams can mess up his entire life. But when it's over, I don't think God will look at him and say, "Tue, tut. He was just junk all along." I think God will cry and say, "He was precious to me. He never really knew who he was."

God's plan and purpose for us is eternal, even when we don't deserve it or see it.

Walking by faith is like using a flashlight. We can't see very far. God doesn't give us the whole plan at once. He gives us a little thirty feet of glow. When we walk that far, then we can see another thirty feet. Faith is committing to walk with Him as far as we can see.

Heaven knows, I don't know. But because heaven knows, I

don't have to . I can stumble around in the fog below simply because I know the sun shines in a bright blue sky above.

"Now when these things begin to take place, *look up*," Jesus said. When I think of Kate now, I look up and remember saying, "Heaven knows, Kate." I still say it, but now, I leave out the comma and announce it as a statement of faith. Heaven knows Kate.